THE WAY WITHIN

Your Path to Enlightenment

Stop Seeking, Start Seeing and Be Awakened

JAMES CAPRA

Spirit Brew Publishing

THE WAY WITHIN - YOUR OWN PATH TO ENLIGHTENMENT

Book 1

Stop Seeking, Start Seeing and be Awakened.

How to transcend your ego, drop the past, leave the future and be free of your thoughts so that you can embrace abundance, enjoy mindfulness, welcome fate and live a liberated happy life of awareness, love, peace and oneness.

January 3rd, 2019, Version 1.1

James Capra

Published by Spirit Brew, Copyright 2019 Spirit Brew Publishing

http://www.SpiritBrew.com

http://www.WayWithin.com

ISBN: 978-1-947326-07-1 (eBook)

ISBN: 978-1-947326-08-8 (Print)

ISBN: 978-1-947326-09-5 (Audio)

Please give this book to someone that needs it, don't hang onto it.

Table of Contents

PREFACE

THE WAY WITHIN

SOON AFTER I started to write the 'Way Within' it became clear there should be two books. One book that deals with awakening and a second book that tackles how to live an awakened life. This, the first book deals with seeing who you are, it's a guide to self-realization. It deals with awaking to your truth, exploring what is meant by enlightenment, and it deals with knowing. The second book deals with living a good life, it's about being authentic, it addresses being and wisdom.

The 'Way Within' has been transformational for me and in a multitude of other guises it has been a catalyst for earlier sages. It's not for everyone but if I have done my job well as a writer and what I'm sharing resonates with you, then you'll quickly get over yourself and find peace, purpose and happiness in life.

The essence of self-realization is that it is a non-verbal and non-emotional experience. The paradox is that after seeing your true nature a myriad of feelings will arise, and naturally most of us try to frame the awakening experience in words. However, regardless of the feelings and words the journey is only ever a discovery of your true self. Of this self only you are an expert, and for reasons we will discuss later, this experience is always beyond words. A trap that keeps many seekers from 'finding' is that they are more attached to words and explanations than they are to the simple knowing of their truth.

Only you can know your truth. So, as you read this book don't cling to my words or doubt yourself when your experience and feelings are different from what other people have described. What you will see will not be what you have imagined and hoped for. It will be far more ordinary and yet at the same time more wonderful than you could imagine. Don't worry if your words are not as poetic or as wise sounding as the mystics. What matters on this journey is that you attend to what you experience and that you don't get distracted by what someone else may write or say.

We use words to communicate, but words are never the thing. I might talk about spacious capacity, you might talk about openness and your true self. Be free of these words, the words don't matter. What matters is that you look for yourself, what matters is that you embrace your true nature and connect with what 'is' and drop what 'is not'.

In these pages I shine a light on challenges that are universal to all seekers. This book is a pot of honey, and as Winnie the Pooh teaches us you can't put your paw in a pot of honey without something good sticking to you.

The "Way Within" has illuminated my life. If you look with me, you'll find the very same light is within you. Once you find your own light you will have no real use for me or this book and you will start to be a lantern that brings light to others.

Love and Light

James Capra,
New York,
August 10th, 2018

WHY READ THIS BOOK?

HAPPINESS, PEACE AND LIBERATION

DO YOU WANT to be happy, do you want to be at peace, do you want to be in harmony with the universe, do you want to know the truth and live authentically? I suspect that you want all of this and you also want to be connected to your life's purpose.

If you want to live a life of peace and happiness, free from stress, fear and illusion. If you want to do the right thing at exactly the right time, then read on. If you want to live in the 'now' then you've come to the right place, and now is the right time for you. If your efforts to change yourself and improve your life have fallen somewhat short of your dreams, then help is at hand. If the old programs, courses, books, teachers, practices or plans haven't permanently solved your problems, then rest assured the 'Way Within' offers the required transformation. A transformation that is both instantaneous and enduring.

FINDING YOUR OWN PATH

This book is not here to teach you anything. It's here to help you to understand the journey in front of you. Your path is uniquely yours. It's not my trip and it's not anyone else's journey either. This book is about walking your own path. Before you start, you need to understand that if you're going to walk your own path, you must stop following other people's footsteps.

The truth is that no one can tell you which is the 'right' path and no one can lead you a single step along the way. This book doesn't tell, it points. This books method is to get you to wake up and look for yourself, look at what's right in front of you, then follow where life is leading!

Life is right in front of you. Life is the only guide you need, life is the only guide there is! However, life is a choice, you must choose and live your own life.

MYSTIC TRUTH

All down the ages there have been mystics that pointed at the same truth. The clue is that they have always been pointing at the truth. They've never said what the truth is or asked people to study their words. They've never said do as they do, they've never said do anything. They've never said look at them and they certainly didn't demand that we hold them in awe. They've not suggested we follow their steps or copy their actions, though for many ardent seekers mimicry has been the course they tried to navigate.

No, the mystics challenged us to look for ourselves. The key is that only you can look for yourself! The mystic truth is only ever about us. It is our truth. You can't find the answer anywhere other than within.

The 'Way Within' is about discovering how to see beyond the mystics and their pointing finger to the secret that is hidden behind the veil of your own mind. It enables you to answer the mystic question, "Who Am I?"

SEEING AND AWARENESS

The 'Way Within' is about opening your eyes. As you start to see, you'll begin to wake up. Awareness grows in you as you wake up, as awareness grows, it re-kindles your innate sense of direction. Only awareness will give you the confidence, motivation and vision to get home. Awareness is what you need if you want to follow where life leads.

The sooner you embrace awareness, the sooner you'll realize that there is only your own path home. The sooner you start to seriously navigate your own path, the sooner you'll come alive to all that life can offer.

Awareness is not a means to an end, it is simultaneously the light that reveals your path and the end that you seek.

THE WAY WITHIN

This book is much more than words or the ideas behind the words. To help you on your journey it will introduce you to some simple tools and techniques that help you to see where you are. Things that will help you to know where you're going, and to sense when and where you are going wrong.

Once you're underway, these same tools will get you to your destination by the shortest of paths. This is the 'Way Within'.

The 'Way Within' is a pathless path. It's an inner way. In practical terms, your journey spans no distance and so requires no movement. The 'Way Within' is a catalyst to instant transformation, it's a direct path.

Once you grasp the way you will be transformed. The good news is that with a little openness on your part you will easily have grasped the 'Way Within' by the end of this book.

PROBLEMS AND YOUR CHOICES

WHICH WAY SHOULD YOU GO?

THERE ARE ONLY two directions available to you in your quest for happiness and success, the outer way or the inner way and only one of these ways delivers true happiness and success.

IMPROVE YOURSELF (THE OUTER WAY)

The first choice, the outer way is all about making something of yourself in the world. It's about improving and developing your personality so that you can go head to head with the strongest personalities and win.

This approach assumes that life is a competition you either win or lose. It supposes there is only so much to go around, and you must grab yours and hang onto it.

The outer way assumes that success is to be found in the world, and that happiness depends on the acquisition of things and experiences, and the avoidance of the things you fear. The outer way is dualistic in nature and positions you as the subject and the things that you seek as objects that can be possessed by your separate self.

This philosophy is born of a sense of lack. The separate self perceives itself as incomplete. When you identify as a separate being, you are driven to make yourself whole. The obvious way to make yourself whole is the get stuff to fill the void in your life the other tactic is to seek experiences as these distract you from the thought that you lack completeness.

According to the outer way to succeed in the world you need tenacity, you need to be positive, and you need to bounce back from all disappointments. You need to keep pushing on if you're going to make your dreams come true. You need to be a better 'you' if you're going to get and keep the things that you believe will make you happy.

The outer way is about what you don't have, it's future focused, however in the end, it's fruitless and exhausting. This is the way most of us take. This is society's way. Fake it until you make it. Be other than you are. Want things to be other than they are. Imagine better, be something else, be someone else!

BE YOURSELF (THE INNER WAY)

For the second way, the inner way, you need to discover who you are and then live authentically. It's consistent with what the ancient Chinese called Tao. Tao is nothing other than your true nature, your very own true and featureless and impossible to lose truth.

The second way is about the now and living in that moment. This way is invigorating and satisfying, and it is the source of all bliss and lasting happiness. The inner way assumes abundance, it never clings because it is forever giving.

The truth that we are pointing towards is the always so, it's the abundance that is to be found at our center. To know yourself as this spacious capacity is to have room for everything, and to rely on yourself is to rely on the only power that is real. You just need to see your truth and live it.

The inner way is unifying. It is born of the enlightening realization that you are not what you thought you were. Once you have grasped your true nature the notion of a separate self and the concept of 'me' falls away and with it the struggle, pain and fear that have shaped so much of your life are dropped to be replaced by peace, happiness and awareness.

This way is not a means to an end, yet it is an end to all seeking.

It's about knowing yourself not just through awareness but as awareness. It's the call to being. It's making a stand as awareness and living authentically.

Awakening to your true nature is not an end to your spiritual work partly because awakening operates at the level of 'knowing'. Knowing is not the end because before we come to knowing, a life time of other beliefs has been recorded at a deep, some might say cellular level and it takes time before you are free of your legacy beliefs and all the associated fear and pain. You must work through your beliefs, but this is easier work when done in the light of awareness.

The inner way brings you to openness and acceptance of what 'is' but it is not be confused with weakness. It takes strength to stay present and then act as the moment requires not as your thoughts and feelings dictate.

THE INDIRECT PATH

If you have decided to adopt the inner way, then your other big choice is between a direct or an indirect path. Most spiritual traditions are indirect paths. The "Way Within" is a direct path.

Indirect paths work like a series of stepping stones that become a path. Each stepping stone is presented as if it's part of the desired goal, when in fact each step is just a device to move you away from where you are. From a position of awareness, you can see that each step is an illusion replacing an illusion. One problem is that the ardent seeker adopts each step as if it's an 'end-in-itself', and the seeker easily gets attached to the steps, making progress impossible.

The method of the indirect path is to continually shed layers of belief, and to drop attachments so that the seeker is elevated (bit by bit) through levels of awareness until with grace the devoted seeker finally falls into enlightenment. The problem is that rarely, if ever, is the person who advocates an indirect path clear about how this final transformation is to be achieved. A transformation that is, it seems, in the lap of the Gods!

Another problem is that as quickly as the seeker sheds old beliefs and drops attachments they pick up new ones.

The indirect path points to what is wrong, divides us, highlights what is at fault and sets us in opposition to evil. The evil is to be found in our body, our thoughts, the ego, the world, our desires, our enemies all of which need to be overcome.

The indirect path is yogic in nature. By yogic I mean that it requires dedication and fortitude, and it requires attention and mastery of all its branches and levels. The nature of an indirect path means that you can't skip straight to the profound understanding, you can't avoid all the bends in the road. You can't save the bends in the road for later when you have learnt to drive and can enjoy them all. No, with the indirect path you must suffer to be free, you must endure trials and challenges that prove your worthiness.

The indirect path typically uses devices like mantras, prayers, rituals, sacrament, sacred objects, physical exercise or sounds to narrow the focus of attention. These objects are tactics to tame the troublesome mind by giving it a single thought to occupy it until with grace, this single thought fades and the seekers attention rests finally in awareness. The practices of the indirect path require mastery on the part of the seeker to progress to the next step. Each step presents a new practice to master.

The indirect path treats attention like elastic because it stretches the seekers attention to its very limit in the hope that when the seeker finally let's go of the objects of their attention their attention will snap like elastic all the way back so that the seeker comes to center where their true self is finally found.

THE DIRECT PATH

The 'Way Within' is a direct path. It brings your attention straight to your true nature and enables you to see free of all illusions. It doesn't hide behind illusions or dabble in halfway house explanations. It gets you to look for yourself, to know for yourself. This is the essence of Tantra, and the 'Way Within' is Tantric and not Yogic in its nature.

The problem that seekers face is that they are seeking and as such imagine themselves to be separate from what they seek. The mystic points to the truth, rather than directly expressing it, exactly because the truth can't be understood by a separate mind. From the perspective of a limited separate mind one can never grasp the truth of our nature, which is limitless and whole.

Therefore the 'Way Within' starts with seeing not looking. We start with seeing so that you can have a direct experience of your true nature. You can't get to your true nature by thinking as a separate mind, but you can know it by seeing. You can have a first-person experience of yourself as the aware space in which all things unfold. Once you experience awareness, which is your Tantra nature, you can let go of your attachment to your separate self. Put simply only after you see yourself as awareness can you drop the belief that you are a separate mind in a body.

This Tantra self knows no difference and it knows no evil. For the Tantra self is one, there is nothing to be beaten, nothing to be judged, nothing to be improved, nothing to be done and no activity. Your true self is aware, whole and wholesome! Awareness is never passive it's always about action, it's about aware action not unaware reaction.

The beauty of the direct path is that there is no need to overcome your past, no need to first master anything or to fix yourself. The truth is that you are not what you think. You are already perfect, you lack nothing other than the knowing of your truth.

The good news is that in the light of awareness the illusions of imperfection, the feelings of need, and all sense of inadequacy fall away.

PEACE, LOVE AND FREEDOM IS WITHIN

Your choice then is to either draw on the well that never runs dry or to try to create your own well. With the inner way, you have all. With the outer way, you are always striving for something else and yet never quite getting it.

Most people come to the second way, the 'Way Within' once they have exhausted the 'Outer Way'. Mostly, people turn to the 'Way Within' after they have broken themselves trying to be something in the world and they are exhausted from fighting to keep something of the world.

It's only from within that you can find the peace and happiness that you crave. From without, you see only fleeting shadows that keep slipping through your grasping fingers.

The 'Way Within' fills you with light and energy. Once you are on this inner path, you'll quickly discover that what you need always flows to and through you. The outer path is dark and drains you of all life and vitality.

The choice is yours. Love and set free what is loved or take what you desire and hold onto it. Let it go to have it or hold it and lose it. This is the divine paradox! This book offers a solution to the paradox, it asks you to choose and then navigate the inner way, the 'Way Within'.

EXPERIENCING WHO YOU ARE

Down the ages the mystics have repeatedly directed us to the question of "Who Am I"? A question which they tell us is the key to enlightenment. Of course, they've also pointed out that enlightenment is beyond words and can't be obtained.

We will tackle the question of "Who Am I?" However, not with more teaching. I'm not going to tell you the answer, how can I? After all, the answer is beyond words.

The truth can only ever be experienced, experienced yes, uttered never! I don't have any answers. However, I will show you how to experience awareness for yourself so that you can see your own truth. That is the answer you need. You need first-person experience of your true nature not second-hand platitudes.

THE WAY TO AWARENESS

This book is here to guide you to awareness. It's here to help you to embrace the insight that awareness is what you are. Awareness is what we all are, it is all that there is, it is all that there ever will be, and awareness is all that there ever was. The book is going to get you to look within and form your own understanding of your true nature based on experience rather than learning or assumptions.

The point the mystics have been making is not about learning anything. Their intension was to get us to experience what 'is' for ourselves, to know what 'is' from awareness and know it as awareness.

The 'Way Within' is blindingly obvious once grasped. The discovery of your inner nature and the truth it brings will illuminate your world. This book is a journey to your core and from there and there alone you will know the truth of "Who Am I?"

The challenge, is to avoid getting caught by a single word in this book, let the words wash over you and then drain away. The trick is to take the journey for yourself, the trick is to look for yourself.

PEACEFUL CENTER

Once you come to your core you can look out from your center, look out from your openness, look from your capacity for life and know the whole truth. Once you come home, once you are centered, you swap fear and pain for peace and happiness. From your center, no one and nothing can ever disturb your peace of mind.

The wholeness that you'll come to know is your essence. This wholeness is what no one can express in words. Wholeness can never be thought, no one can think it, and it can never be taught as knowledge. No one can teach or learn about wholeness. All is not lost because the wholeness we seek is right here right now for anyone that looks and sees for themselves. For the seer wholeness will be theirs forever.

CHOOSING THE QUALITY OF YOUR LIFE

The quality of your life is a product of the choices you make and the paths you take. The 'Way Within' will bring an end to all your fruitless meandering. It brings total clarity so that you can make the right choices. It illuminates the path before you so that you can go forwards in peace and with purpose. There is no greater quality of life than the truth you'll discover through the 'Way Within.'

The 'Way Within' brings you home to yourself and you will know yourself for the first time.

REMOVE THE STRESS FROM YOUR LIFE

Every 'thing' is under stress because all things are subject to forces that push and pull them in different directions. Every single body in the universe is constantly subject to the influence of every other thing in the universe, from the farthest star to the nearest particle, they all exert forces on each other.

As a body, you feel stress as the universe pushes and pulls you. If that wasn't pressure enough, you feel even more stress as all that you are is forced into the confined space that is your body.

Logically, the only way to be free of stress is to get so small that you are nothing or get so large that you encompass all things. What if by some magic, you could be at the same time both nothing and all things then you'd be doubly blessed. Guess what, you are doubly blessed, you just don't see it yet. The 'Way Within' brings your blessings into focus and removes all stress.

FIRST STAND AS AWARENESS

The aim of the 'Way Within' is to enable you to see for yourself how you are both 'nothing' and all things. You're the nothing from which all things spring and the infinite emptiness in which all things reside.

The first challenge is to see yourself as the space of awareness, to stop seeing yourself as a separate mind-body that has awareness. The challenge is to stand as awareness.

In awareness, you are not your thoughts, feelings, fears, beliefs or even your body or mind. Once this realization is achieved the 'Way Within' reveals how to live from awareness. This takes a little effort because the old feelings of being a mind in a body take both time and awareness to dissolve. The old feelings linger for quite a while after the initial realization, the good news is that they can't last once you embrace the knowing of awareness.

Your challenge, and the great opportunity I'm bringing you, is to live life by what you will see. In other words, to live your life by what you are, and to never again be stressed by what you are not. This is what I mean by standing in awareness. This is peace, this is love, and this is what you are, love and peace.

FINAL STEP - EMBRACE ONENESS

This book deals with the challenge of standing in awareness. However, there is a final challenge which is how to let go of the lingering sense of separation.

Seekers will often accept the notion of being awareness while still hanging onto a lingering sense of being the subject (awareness) in which objects appear. Many people equate the view that they are the awareness in which all things appear as being non-dualistic. However, clearly if there is a subject and objects this is a sort of dualism.

The 'Way Within' reveals that this is an illusion and that the truth runs far deeper. The knowing that we are moving towards can be summed up as oneness.

The next book moves you towards an ever deeper knowing of yourself as awareness. When you embrace yourself as the knowing of awareness all separation finally dissolves as awareness collapses into itself.

WHICH PATH SHOULD YOU TAKE?

A confusing problem we seekers face when we set off on life's journey is that there are paths, paths and more paths. Along the way, you will find people who will keenly tell you which way to go. Everyone seems to have an opinion and any path will get you somewhere. However, there's only one path for you and that's your own path. You can spend a lifetime on another person's path and get somewhere else but never home. Be warned, when you take another's path, each step you take will keep you away from your true destination.

Remember, those that know won't say and those that say don't know!

Some paths will give you glimmers of what you'd hoped for, though in the end even the glittering paths will leave you stranded. These glimmers will leave you lustful for another glimpse, seeking another taste of the bliss that you long for.

The nature of enlightenment is binary, you're either enlightened or you're not. With enlightenment, it's on or it's off, there is no half way house in this game, you can't be a bit awake. There are no half Buddha's. Likewise, there are no half-way paths to enlightenment.

You've probably come to believe that all valuable paths, are long and hard. It's scary to think that for the one true path that's going the right way there are infinitely more paths leading you in the wrong direction.

YOUR OWN PATH

Don't be put off. In awareness, there's only your own path. The problem is that most of the time and for most of us, this path is lost in all the noise of life and the noise of others. The 'Way Within' delivers the quiet space you need and from which you'll find your awareness and clarity.

Awareness and clarity make it impossible to get lost again. Of course, from time to time you will still wander from your true course, but when you do stray, you'll quickly realize your error and naturally correct your heading.

If you follow your own path with awareness you will be pleasantly surprised because the 'Way Within' is not nearly as long or as hard as you'd feared. The direct path of awareness is a path on no distance and takes no time to complete. So, you can drop the belief about your path having to be long, hard and scary!

FIRST-HAND EXPERIENCE, NOT SECOND-HAND KNOWLEDGE

If you want to get to Nirvana and you want to get there now rather than waiting a life-time, then follow the exercises in this book. By follow, I mean do them. Don't just read them. Reading the exercises will do nothing.

If you want to come home to find Nirvana, then you need to experience awareness first hand. Don't crudely ape what some guru did or people claim he or she did. This way is all about experience. It's never about words, concepts, mimicry or ritual.

Enlightenment is first-person singular. You must see it for yourself, but when you do it is seen in oneness not in separateness. You don't get enlightened. Rather, you awake to what we all already are, you wake to what awareness is. You wake to what you are.

You can't have enlightenment. It's not a thing. It's not an attribute of who you are. You are an attribute of awareness, a modulation, a ripple in its ocean. Like a current in the ocean, there is no separation between you, the current, and the ocean of awareness. You are born of awareness's emptiness, shimmer for a bit in its light before merging back into its fathomless depth.

Enlightenment is just the knowing of your true nature as awareness. It's experiencing yourself as awareness instead of thinking that you are a mind in a body. When we say, we awake, we mean we wake from the old dream of our self as a separate self. We wake into awareness.

We wake together, into oneness. We wake without having to move an inch or change a thing in our life. Without adding a thing!

The point of the exercises in this book is to allow you to gain first-hand experience of your true nature. The 'Way Within' is about giving you the experience you need to see yourself so that you can drop the notion that you are a separate self.

So, do the exercises, get the experience and swap my words for the personal insight that will allow you to see your own path. Then, and only through your own first-person experience, you'll come to awareness.

You must see for yourself. You must make your own way from here. No one can tell you. Sorry to labor the point, but you really don't need more rituals, or more practices. You don't need holy things, or robes. You don't need hats, books or even mantras. You just need awareness so that you can see the light and walk forwards into it.

THE GREATEST GIFT

If you haven't got deep pockets to pay for courses or the time to go on endless retreats, then you're in luck, as the 'Way Within' won't cost a penny and takes very little time to realize.

The 'Way Within' is a gift, the greatest gift and because it's a gift there is nothing owed. You need to receive this gift with humility and gratitude. These are pre-requisites, you will also need to drop a few illusions along the way.

NO SACRIFICES REQUIRED

If concerns for the practicalities of life like your loved ones and work have been stopping you from pursuing your deepest desires; drop that thought. You really don't need to worry because apart from a few stolen moments reading the book and a little time doing the exercises, the rest of your life can carry on unhindered.

The 'Way Within' is an end to all suffering, and liberation from suffering can't be realized through suffering. In awareness, you will never set out to cause suffering in others. If you do set out to cause suffering, you're not in awareness.

This doesn't mean that those nearest you won't suffer. However, their suffering isn't because of your awakening. If they do suffer it will be down to their fears not your awakening. It will be down to their desire for things to be other than they are, for you to be other than you are. People generally don't want transformation, they want the familiar. They typically want what they had before. They want you back to how you were because after an awakening you no longer fit in the box they have for you. Once you cease to fit into the boxes people have for you, once you stop behaving how they want or stop believing what they believe you become a threat to the order that they are striving to maintain.

SAVE YOURSELF FIRST

One dilemma you will have to overcome is the necessity to save yourself first. The necessity of putting your own awakening before those you love, putting your salvation before those you wish most dearly to save.

You can't save anyone if you stay asleep. Paradoxically, you also can't save anyone even when you are awake. However, with awareness you can point the way. You can become a beacon of love and light that inspires people and helps them to find their own path. You can be wide open to all possibility and say "Yes" to life.

Sadly, those you love the most can find it hardest to see the light as they are looking for something else. Often it is your loved ones that are unable to be present with you because they are prone towards dwelling in the past or hoping for a future that rekindles their history.

THE EXTRAORDINARY DOING OF NOT DOING

In awareness, you can't neglect the practicalities of life. Rather, you'll stop doing things and instead they will be done. There will be less resistance and less effort.

In awareness, there will be doing. However, there will be no you that is doing the doing.

You'll still pick up the kids from school, go to the park, do the shopping, take out the bins and do the dishes only now all these things are done mindfully. No more chores, no more boredom, no more bitterness or regret. Where there is boredom, chores, bitterness, fears, regrets, then there is no awareness.

For the sage even blinking his eyes is too much effort, eyes are blinked!

RESULTS THAT LAST

The 'Way Within' is not about change, it's about transformation, and transformation unlike change is instant and enduring.

Once you have known the truth there's no denying it, your course is set and from here on in there's no doubt that you will increasingly live from awareness.

The 'Way Within' doesn't just reacquaint you with your true nature. It forces you to embrace your vital role in nature. Once you've glimpsed a little of this there is no turning back, you will keep going forwards. This is not a question of grace it is just a question of seeing yourself as awareness and accepting this is what you are. Infinite and eternal. Not separate, not mind, not body, not limited and not mortal. It's a question of mindful living.

THE LEGACY OF SEPERATENESS

After you have awoken, you will know yourself as awareness. However, even after the life changing revelation that you are awareness, it turns out that your journey is far from being at an end.

This is where the work starts as the old feeling of being a separate mind and body lingers. These feelings may be hollow, but they will keep hanging around and arising. Your work now is not to remove these lingering feelings and thoughts, your work is to let them arise in awareness and openness without any resistance, know them for what they really are. With the simple knowing and your acceptance they finally lose their power over you.

MASTER THE NOW

The 'Way Within' reveals that all the paths are an illusion, as is time itself. It also helps you to master the 'now', where you will learn to remove the biggest road block that stands in your way. The road block in question is you, you are the only real obstacle. It's only ever what you think and how you use attention that keeps you from complete peace of mind.

A big part of what this book offers is the direct experience of nature, and it's this experience that ensures you fully appreciate that there's only one 'now.' This is the experience of the 'eternal now', the 'holy instant'. The 'Way Within' enables you to get over yourself so that you can enjoy the 'now.' Only in the 'now' can you embrace the truth and enjoy a life truly lived.

WHY IS IT ALL GOING SO WRONG?

Everywhere I go and everywhere I look I see people struggling with life. The struggling I witness is a direct consequence of how people experience the world. The struggle arises because we experience the world as a reflection of our conscious mind and the thoughts we linger on.

We have all experienced times when life goes sublimely well, then something changes and with a single event everything changes. Suddenly, you can't recapture the good times again.

At times, it may seem like life is against us. At these times it feels, looks and sounds like we are our own worst enemy. For many of us it's like we've lost our way. It's like we're no longer connected to life in a meaningful way.

How would it be if you were at peace and had peace of mind in all situations? How would it be if you were not troubled by what you thought or by what happened? How would it be if you were able to live in and from the 'now'? How would life be if you had awareness?

I'm here to help you to see into yourself so that you can know that there's nothing wrong with the world or with the people around you. The fault is not in the stars, the fault is in what you choose to think about them.

SEEKERS

Most people would relish finding a solution to the problem of life and how to live a peaceful, harmonious, happy and productive life. Some of us are actively looking for peace, happiness, fulfilment, bliss, enlightenment and God.

While we're seeking a solution, we also want answers. We are looking to heal our lives, improve our bodies, enhance our skills, and correct our behaviors. Some of us are madly trying to defeat our ego or drop the self.

We want to know what, how, when and who? We are looking for something else, sometime else or someone else. The 'Way Within' is an end to seeking, it is about finding and being.

REFLECTION ON AN END TO SEEKING

Take a moment and reflect what your life would be if you found yourself perfect, peaceful, happy, open and love filled. How would it be if you swapped the strain of trying to change what you are, if you exchanged the trauma of trying to change what is happening for the readiness to act as life requires with no resistance?

I'm not asking you to give up seeking, I'm not telling you to act as needed in the moment with no resistance, I'm just asking, would that be a good life? How would that feel?

I'M OK, YOU'RE NOT OK

All too often we put in real effort to appear OK. However, the truth is that deep down most of us are dissatisfied with the reality of our lives. We're disappointed with our situation and with our relationships.

Most of us are channeling huge amounts of energy into a charade of trying to be someone in the world. We're trying to be someone else, trying to at least appear OK. However, trying to appear successful and happy is exhausting. Appearing OK is a game that's not worth playing. You can't win. It's a game that denies reality and impairs your potential.

We're also insanely trying to make other people be other than they are. We are busy trying to change reality to fit our idea of what it should be. We are disappointed because life is not how we want it to be, people are not how we want them to be and we're not how we want to be.

Most of us have got so good at the charade we have come to believe it. We have hidden our dissatisfaction from the world in general and from ourselves in particular.

We are dissatisfied because we are comparing our fictional character with an error. The error that things should be other than they are. This error is not just exhausting, it's totally nuts and totally unnecessary as you'll come to realize before you finish this book. The truth will set you free!

THE TRAP OF POSITIVE THINKING

THE PROBLEMS OF POSITIVE THINKING

IN A WAY, positive thinking and the 'Way Within' are two opposing approaches, though they can both be effective at opening positive energy in our lives.

Positive thinking works but only on one level. It's a brilliant technique for overcoming many of the obstacles in your life. Those problems which stem from your negative thoughts about yourself and your environment.

Positive thinking is applicable to the outer way, not the inner way. It's about making yourself better. A better thing in the world.

The difference is that with the 'Way Within' you are essentially trying to 'un-thing' yourself, to be open to what 'is' to drop the 'me' and reveal the truth of who you are so that you can be at ease and free.

With positive thinking, you are trying to rethink yourself. You are putting on a new face. With positive thinking, you are creating a story of who you are. You are extending, enhancing and polishing the 'me'. You are projecting yourself boldly into the world. You are creating a thing of yourself and your perspective is as an object in a world of objects.

Whereas, with the 'Way Within' you are taking your face off. You are 'un-thinging' yourself, 'un-selfing' yourself.

Positive thinking is just kicking the can down the road. The thing with kicking the can down the road is that sooner or later you're going to have to give it another kick, normally after you've picked up the pieces from the last kick!

In contrast with the 'Way Within' you are finally seeing that you are not a player is a story. You're no mere can kicker. You are the boundless loving space within which all stories are played and out of which all objects are made. You are the space which is never corrupted by any narrative or character. You are the space that is aware of what unfolds and aware of itself as the space. Your perspective on life is neither as the subject nor as an object. You are also both subject and object. You are the awareness from which all arises and into which all returns.

AUTHENTIC THINKING

When I talk about the problem of positive thinking I mean that it is positive thinking that is keeping you from authenticity. This is a big yet subtle problem.

The problem is made worse because positive thinking can be used to create a good story. In fact, with affirmations that are based on sound spiritual insights, you can create a story that is close to the truth of who you are.

No matter how appealing the story may be, we can never be authentic and truthful when what we 'are' is a fiction. Not even a beautiful and spiritual fiction is ever going to lead to your true self.

We are never authentic when we are derived by creating an illusion! No matter how good a story is, it is not the truth.

No words or story can capture the truth of your majesty. In this game, you can't fake it until you make it. You can't think your way to ultimate glory. The 'Way Within' is about seeing the truth and loving what 'is'.

The 'Way Within' is about seeing that you are not your thoughts. It's NOT about picking which thoughts will define you. It's about NOT about getting rid of the thoughts you don't like.

Ask yourself, is it better to try to fake it until you make it? Ask yourself, is it better to live a hallucination? Ask yourself, is it not instead better to personally see 'who' you truly are and to know for yourself the truth that all is well, you are well and all things are well?

AUTHENTIC SEEING

If you really want to see for yourself, you must understand that you can't see clearly if you are putting anything between you and the world.

Can you get to the truth by masking illusion with delusion? Ask yourself what you hope to gain by faking it?

GAINING ENLIGHTENEMENT

It's important that you understand that you can't gain enlightenment if you are not prepared to see the truth, drop the illusions, drop the stories. Fakes, never awake. The paradox is that you can't get enlightened because the very act of seeking objectifies enlightenment which in turn automatically puts it beyond reach.

Ask yourself is this search for enlightenment really an ego game and do you really want to play it? Ask yourself, who is the ultimate winner of ego games? See how the ego is maintained by playing a game that you can never win.

POSITIVE THINKING BARS TRUE HAPPINESS

Regardless of what you think is better, positive thinking always has the lingering specter of insecurity lurking in the wings. For sure, positive thinking is an effective band aid. However, in the end it's only dealing with the symptoms. It's just covering up your perceived shortcomings.

Positive thinking makes changes to the 'me', but the 'me' is an illusion. 'Me' is just an old story you have been telling the world about who you are.

Positive thinking can make deeper changes to your beliefs and world view, but you will always be vulnerable to negative thinking. You'll be vulnerable even when you're not having a negative thought. You're vulnerable because in the back of your mind is the fear that you will sooner or later have negative thoughts, the fear that you will lose what has been gained by your positive thinking.

In contrast, the centered seer can never again be insecure about anything. The seeing sage is no-thing with nothing to fear and nothing to lose. The seeing sage is just love, peace and contentment.

The 'Way Within' starts with 'seeing'. However, being a seer is only the first step. Next, we should live from awareness as a sage, which is a life's work. A good life!

GUARD AGAINST OPTIMISM AND PESSIMISM

Talking of positive thinking reminds me of another trap that the unwary seeker can fall into, the trap of optimism. I'm particularly prone to this and I'm equally susceptible to the related trap of pessimism.

Seekers often overtly eschew bad karma and seek out only good karma. While at a subconscious level they may be drawn to the bad.

The 'Way Within' frees you from all karma.

Both pessimism and optimism are illusory states that are pursued by the unaware. In both cases, we corrupt reality by either embellishing it with undue light or tainting events with unnecessary darkness.

The optimist imagines everything in beautiful colors. For him the sad events in life must be dressed up in idealistic projections.

The optimist is forever trying to promote and maintain harmony much to the detriment of his own life force. It's all an act, driven by his imagination but with effects that reach the world at large. The optimist is escaping reality, striving for beauty. Paradoxically, because of his efforts he misses the true beauty in the world.

However, the pessimist you could argue is in a worse place. His is darkness, worries and tears. His imaginings turn the most insignificant events into dramas that torture him, and if he can, he'll torture those around him with his nightmarish visions.

The effects of both attitudes can be detrimental to the physical body, leading to stress and denying the body the health and vitality that flows from awareness. The solution is not more thinking or even different thinking, the solution is awareness. In the light of awareness all illusions are first seen through and then quietly dropped.

POSITIVE THINKING CAN'T ESCAPE STRESS

Positive thinking may overwhelm some of the thoughts that can lead to stress, but as an object in the world you will always be subject to stress.

Positive thinking will certainly help to displace a previous pessimistic attitude and sooth the related stress that such an attitude creates. However, as you create a bigger, brighter, more dynamic, more successful self, you will find that new stresses emerge. There will be more demands, more expectations and inevitably you'll find that you have more to lose.

Perhaps the greatest stress arises from the sheer effort to keep projecting this positive 'me' into the world. You are quite literally a hell of a plate to keep spinning.

The 'Way Within' enables you to drop all the causes of stress, including those of the physical body. It clears the vision in order that the truth of the present moment can replace fear with peace and love. Critically, this peace is achieved regardless of any external events.

Through the 'Way Within' you'll finally come to know yourself as timeless and infinite instead of as a mortal stress body.

TRANSEND IT DON'T FAKE IT

It's a big assumption that you can 'fake it' then 'make it' and expect lasting results.

In my experience, thoughts will hit you sooner or later that shout all is not well and then before you know it you'll find that all is indeed not well.

With positive thinking, you are never more than a thought away from this 'dis-ease' and even if you're not suffering right now there's always a little nagging fear that you will succumb.

The 'Way Within' leads you through the transcendence of the self so that in time you can assume your role as co-creator. This is the shift you really need. It's not a shift from faking it to making it. No, this is a shift from loving it to being it.

This is the nature and promise of the good life that awaits you if you follow the 'Way Within'.

THE SCIENCE OF AFFIRMATIONS

All through the last century experiments have been undertaken to assess the objective impact of positive thinking. Of these the most interesting and I think the most relevant to our discussion, are those experiments which tested the impact that affirmations have on our performance.

A significant number of these studies have demonstrated again and again that on their own affirmations don't improve performance. Experiments in fact suggest that for our optimum performance, being open to what is, is a good thing. Whereas, being over confident and possessing blind faith in one's ability is detrimental to performance.

For me, the key factor is that affirmations should be used with knowledge and a deeper purpose to co-create what 'is'. Not to mask, change or influence anything. You are here to enable what 'is' not change it. In this way, the 'Way Within' brings you into the 'now'.

POSITIVE THINKING KILLS THE MOMENT

At its essence, I think that these experiments point to the reality that life is fresh and new, and we have to be open to each new moment and treat what 'is' with love and gratitude. We need a readiness to do what is required in the current moment. To do what is needed from you now. Positive Thinking kills the present moment, it kills the 'now' and takes away our ability to do what is required of us in this moment.

You could say that Positive Thinking kills the moment. In other words, because we bring the past with us, and think about the future, we are dead to the moment. Our very hopes and wishes would deny us the beauty and magic that is available right now.

BLIND FAITH IS JUST PLAIN BLIND

It also raises the issue of blind faith. This is another reason why I council you not to have faith in what you read. Don't take what I say on trust, take the time to look for yourself. Test the insights I'm sharing with you, challenge everything. Then, when you look you will arrive at the experience of the truth. You will arrive at your own experience of the truth and this is knowledge worth having!

Clearly, first-person experience is preferable to setting off, yet again, on a way that reveals a world through faith in second-hand knowledge. Second-hand knowledge and faith both promise much but only ever leave you blind to the truth.

UNAWARE AFFIRMATIONS

One problem with affirmations when used without awareness is that they impair your ability to see for yourself. To the un-awakened mind, they add something else between you and reality.

What's more, they also have the corrosive effect of setting your mind to filter out what doesn't agree with your affirmations. Often, what gets missed is exactly what you need to be successful. You end up missing the pointer that says you're heading down the wrong track. You miss the real opportunity of this moment.

Few things are more detrimental to high performance than heading off down the wrong path without the humility to reconsider your course.

MORE CHALLENGES FOR POSITIVE THINKING

While maintaining a positive attitude towards things you may miss the valuable insight that a thing is not worth pursuing or that you might not be able to solve the problem before you. When faced with an intractable problem you are much better served by moving on to the next problem, which you can answer correctly, rather than ploughing on in 'fallow' land. Similarly, if it becomes clear that something won't deliver the promised happiness you've been seeking then clearly another course would be better.

One simple experiment that the positive thinking researchers did brought this home for me. They were testing people's ability to solve relatively simple equations. In the experiment people are split into two groups. The first group is primed to repeatedly tell themselves, both verbally and in their mind, an affirmation to the effect that they can solve the equations. The second group is required to tell themselves that they may struggle with some of the equations.

When both groups are subsequently given the equations, the second group, the doubters performed significantly better than the positive thinkers.

This wasn't a one off. Researchers have conducted lots of variations of the experiments and the results are consistent, which brings into question the wisdom of positive thinking as a solution to life's practical challenges.

Don't worry, we will pick up affirmations again, but only after we have cleared the decks so to speak. I'm not saying affirmations are bad or wrong, I'm saying that maybe you're not yet in the right frame of mind to use them effectively.

POSITIVE VISION NOT BLIND FAITH

I've observed the key influence that positive thinking has in a successful life is to help people create and sustain a positive vision of what they would achieve. Having this vision in mind causes people to move towards this vision. Or more accurately, it enables their vision to move towards them and manifest itself though the Law of Attraction.

Co-creation is our great gift and we are always co-creating. Be careful here, having blind faith in your abilities, especially where this is contrary to your reality, is only ever a bad thing.

Wanting things for egotistical reasons, wanting things so you will feel better or to support a fantasy of who you are is never a good thing. Wanting things for egotistical reasons can only make things worse in the long run. This is always a step away from an enlightened life, a step away from what you truly seek.

The key to success and happiness is aligning our vision with the will of the universe. All that it takes is for you to come home and finally know yourself so that you can go forth fearlessly with love, integrity and authenticity.

DROP AFFIRMATIONS

By extension then, if you have any affirmations, I'm going to encourage you to drop them.

I know that this is a bitter pill for many of you because affirmations, perhaps more than anything else up until now, will have proved themselves a powerful tonic for your woes.

Don't get me wrong, I see all around me the positive benefits of affirmations and I have many friends that use good and powerful affirmations about themselves. Affirmations are often used to good effect in people's lives. I don't say, never use affirmations, what I'm suggesting is that we should first get to know ourselves so that we can learn to live in sympathy with the universe not against it. So that we can embrace the universal flow rather than envisioning the egos goals.

In many cases the affirmations people tell themselves are a close reflection of the truth and they create a vivid picture of their true self. However, they are always that. Always a picture, an approximation, a story. Always somewhat removed from the reality of who we are. It's like worshiping a false idol. If you keep telling yourself "All is well" and "you are well" without knowing that this is true from your own first-person experience, then sooner or later you will come unstuck.

Unfortunately, there's no way around it. If you are going to complete the 'Way Within' you must, in the end, drop the affirmations. If you don't drop your affirmations, you'll never truly know who you are or go on to realize the liberation that the 'Way Within' brings. There's an infinite difference between saying "All is well" and knowing "All is well, all things are well, and all shall be well"!

DON'T PANIC

The thought of dropping your affirmations might be too much for some of you. It's like giving up the life raft and swimming off into the dark empty ocean. If it's too stressful for you now, don't sweat it. Take one step at a time. When you start to see, you will at some point stop needing to tell yourself the old stories. I'm not saying that you will stop telling stories. The process of storytelling will probably never end. However, you'll stop needing them and you'll 'see through' the stories you tell rather than 'seeing' with them!

Don't panic! In fact, don't give affirmations anymore thought for now. If you are a big fan of affirmations and they make up an important part of your routine, or if you feel that they lend you essential shelter from the storm, then don't drop your affirmations just yet. Please don't do anything just because I tell you to. Instead, look at what I'm going to point you towards then make your own mind up.

LETTING GO / GETTING OUT OF THE WAY

Stay with me, affirmations or no affirmations. It won't make any major difference now and it certainly won't stop you from taking the first steps, after which, you'll start to lose the need to have the old affirmations.

Here's my last thought on this then I'll shut up.

The essence of the 'Way Within' is about letting go, it's about getting out of the way. It's about stopping all that meddling in the running of the universe. The 'Way Within' is about letting the universe unfold through you. Having affirmations is a significant bit of hanging on. For the un-awakened mind affirmations are a blatant attempt at trying to run your little part of the universe. Affirmations without awareness are an attempt to bend the will of the universe to your desires. If you follow the 'Way Within' you will undertake the biggest miracle of your life when in full awareness you cede your will to the universal will. You will discover the deeper truth that the universal will is in fact your will and once your will is aligned with the universal will then creation will flow through you.

CO-CREATION NOT EGO-MANIFESTATION

This section will probably be a major source of confusion to many of you as it may seem like the 'Way Within' contradicts itself as it urges you to drop positive thinking and leave your affirmations behind. Yet, it acknowledges the *Law of Attraction* and in the next book we will focus on our ultimate role as co-creator of the universe.

Again, don't sweat it for now. For now, all we must do is look and see. In a way, this first book about seeing is just laying the foundation and starts the process of cleansing so we can become so wide open that the universal will can manifest through us. The will of the universe can only manifest when we co-create on purpose. It's a poor universe we create when we try to manifest a twisted reflection of our ego.

Until we can see clearly and have awareness, any forays into the *Law of Attraction* are going to be attempts to subvert the universe's will to the wants of ego. Whereas through the 'Way Within' you will become one with the universe and its love will flow freely through you. In this way, there will be no ego, or if there is some vestige of ego it will be in the background not running the show.

If you leap into the *Law of Attraction* right now the chances are that all your efforts will be driven by your ego. When the ego is in charge you can be sure little good will come of it. Your thoughts will be about stuff. Your head will be all awash with images of new cars, nicer houses, sun kissed tropical beaches, but this is just more stuff and more experiences. None of this brings anything new, fresh and needed into the world. We don't need another Aston Martin (I'd quite like one though). For this to work we must be open to the void so that new possibilities can be realized from out of the no-thing. You can't do that if your head is bursting with stuff that already exists.

In this book, I'm talking from the point of view of the 'Way Within'. There are other 'Ways' and some of these may embrace co-creation and use the *Law of Attraction*, and they may not require you first to have awareness but instead rely on first-person experience of the *Law of Attraction* to bring you to awareness. Of these ways, I know nothing. What I do know is the 'Way Within' and that is a sure way and direct way to get home and live on purpose.

The choice though is yours about which way you go.

THE PROBLEMS OF SEEKING

This leads us to the problem of seeking. Seeking a better life, seeking a better partner, seeking a better job, seeking a better place to live, seeking a better set of skills, seeking more knowledge, seeking a better understanding, seeking a better body, seeking a greater connectedness to nature or simply seeking a better sense of it all! In fact, for most of us the problem clearly is seeking, seeking, seeking!

The trouble is that all this seeking and the corresponding covering up our perceived shortcomings takes us away from our goal of happiness. We have become seekers of something else, seekers of somewhere else, and seekers of someone else. We try to move towards our goal. However, all movement is taking us away from what we truly seek. Which is only ever what we already are.

We have reduced ourselves into actors in our own TV show. In fact, we are neither seekers nor actors. The truth is that we can't move on until we let go of the search and stop trying to direct the movie of our lives.

Material seeking or spiritual seeking, it's all the same, it's all seeking something other than 'this.' It's always a journey into a future that doesn't exist, a journey that takes us away from the now. It's a search for something in the future for 'me.' It's the 'me' that's at the root of all this searching. Seeking happiness for me, money for me, a job for me, a car for me, friends for me, a wife for me, it's all me, me, me!

The 'Way Within' is a journey to this moment, to 'now'. It's a journey of no distance but once taken all of space and time will be yours in the eternal present. There is no future only the creation of this moment, and all moments are now.

When you are present in awareness, you're not present as 'me' you're present as 'I' and for the 'I' there are no wants and the only desire is to be open to what 'is'.

SEEKING IS ANOTHER KIND OF FLEEING

We constantly use seeking as an antidote to the pressure that the ego places on us, the pressure to be someone in the world. Seeking is an anesthetic that we use to numb the pain of life. Seekers are just like the worker that as soon as he gets paid hits the pub on a Friday night and drinks himself to oblivion. Drinking so that he can escape himself. Drinking so that for a few hours he won't be himself anymore.

Essentially, we are terrified of who we are, or more accurately the ego is terrified of our true nature. The ego doesn't want us to know the truth and so it obscures the truth with petty fears and therefore we prefer a fiction. It's why we prefer to look for happiness out there. It's all because we have become scared of 'who' we are.

The ego puts the fear of God into us because the ego knows that the truth brings destruction to the ego. It makes us so scared that we run from who we are. We are so scared that we run to the bottle, to the charade, to sex, to drugs, to TV, to stuff and always to more 'me.' It's no wonder then that we totally overlook the 'I'.

The ego convinces us to keep seeking happiness anywhere but here and anytime but now. It convinces us that happiness is out there and sets us after something in the future. It gets us seeking something that deep down we know is at best only going to offer us a fleeting reprieve from the pain we feel.

Seeking is a powerful drug, it should be no surprise then that we get hooked. The 'Way Within' is your twelve-step program to liberation, peace, happiness and health. It's the ultimate cure for seekers. Best of all it doesn't have twelve steps, it only has two!

MISSING THE HOLY MOMENT

With all this drama and searching for things for 'me' we have managed to mask the truth of who we really are. It turns out that our perfection, heritage and inheritance is nothing to be feared. However, along the way we've managed to overlook the now and in doing so we miss the beauty of the holy moment.

We've been tricked by the ego and lured from the light to play its insane games. Games that we can never win and that only cause pain and suffering. Whereas, in the holy moment we will find everlasting peace and happiness. Ask yourself, do you doubt for a single moment that you'll find peace and happiness in the 'now'?

Consequently, this is where we are going to look. This is the method of the 'Way Within' to find peace and happiness in the 'now'.

THE EGO'S PLAN FOR HAPPINESS

Somewhere down the line we've all adopted the ego's crazy plan to find happiness.

As you now know, its plan is to seek and never find. The ego's plan is to challenge us to find happiness in the world, the ego is challenging us to find happiness by changing the world or changing the people in the world.

The role of our mind in this plan is to find things outside of ourselves that we need to fix, the mind is also tasked seeking things to 'have', things that will make us happy.

For most of us, this is the essence of all the plans we've been unwittingly following so far in our lives. That's certainly my story. All my plans were to get things or change things 'out there' in the world. Plans to change things so that they met with my idea of what they should be. Even at the times when I was planning to improve myself, the truth was that the improvements were all ultimately aimed at getting things 'out there'. My self-improvement was always superficial and never touched on my true nature. In fact, all my efforts only ever moved me away from the beautiful truth of who I am.

My seeking drove me away from my perfection and turned me into a flawed and fruitless parody of my glorious self.

SEEKERS SEEK BUT THEY NEVER FIND

When someone is a seeker, they always seek with a goal in mind and consequently they only see what they already have in their mind.

Seeking means having a goal. Finding means being free, being open and having no goals. In striving for their next goal, the seeker invariably misses what is always in plain sight.

Seekers look to teachers. They try to master practices, they grasp for words, they try to discern meaning and they try to think great thoughts in the hope that something they try will provide them with the answer. These efforts always fall short because all of this is dualistic, two faced. Whereas the truth is non-dualistic, whole and ironically the seeker is already at one with it all.

It's just the thoughts that occupy the seeking mind that keep the blissful truth at bay. We are already at one with it all, it's just our thoughts that keep us separate.

The truth is not good, the truth is not wise. The truth is both good and bad, it's wise and stupid. When seekers stop seeking they find what they have always been yearning for.

I'm not asking you to stop seeking. I'm just showing you a different perspective and I will leave it with you for now. I'll leave it to incubate for now.

While it incubates ask yourself: What would your life be like without all your seeking? What would your life be like without the endless struggle? What would things be like without the fears and thoughts that rule your life?

FATE, CHAOS, PEACE AND HAPPINESS

Fate unfolds unstoppable. For most people, for seekers, fate operates outside of them and brings chaos then death. For the wise, for seers, fate rises from within and becomes the source of an eternal life of peace and happiness.

The ego's plan for happiness, this relentless search for happiness out there in the world, places people at the mercy of fate.

The 'Way Within' brings you home. It brings you to the place you have never really left; a place where fate and fortune count for nothing. The mastery of fate is unlike any mastery you've experienced before. It arises not from control, it arises from acceptance and love. Fate's revelation is oneness.

WHAT'S SO DIFFERENT ABOUT THIS BOOK?

Unlike self-help books, this book is not about change. As you read this book you don't need to change a thing about yourself, not even after you've read it.

You don't have to change anything about your situation. Indeed, one of the key messages is that you must avoid changing anything. Be aware, yes. Observe events and observe yourself because these are all important to the transformation on offer. So, instead of tinkering with what's troubling you, you need to learn to just watch and leave things as they are.

The 'Way Within' offers you the chance to transform your life, no changes required. This is not about adjusting yourself and improving your circumstances. Instead, it's about embracing yourself and loving all that life offers, and the good news is that life offers all you really desire!

If you adopt the 'Way Within' and work with this book, your path will become clear and when you are ready your transformation will come. It'll come in an instant and it'll be easily achieved by anyone who follows the directions and looks for themselves. It comes to anyone that makes up their minds based on examined truth and is open to and embraces the truth of what is seen.

AN INEFFABLE MESSAGE

It's ironic reading a book that can't tell you anything. A book where the essential point you need to grasp can never be explained. I hope that you now appreciate that nobody can tell you the answers that you've been seeking. If you grasp just this for now that is a major step forwards!

Instead of giving you any answers, the 'Way Within' points to the insight you need so that you can go and know the truth. So that you can experience the truth for yourself.

Words don't matter, they have no value. What matters is what is being pointed at. What's important is what is being revealed and the key to its revelation is experiencing it for yourself.

You'll just have to look where the book is pointing. You must be very careful not to get caught looking at the book and then mistaking its words for what they reveal.

Be warned, because this is the trap of all mystic teachings and this is the heart of all religion. Heart is perhaps the wrong word. The start or foundation of all religion is perhaps nearer the truth. All religion is based on mistaking the pointing finger for what is being pointed at. Religion makes the finger into a sacred relic and for the faithful, the finger becomes more important than what is beyond the finger. For the faithful the finger becomes more important even than the person the finger is pointing at. For the faithful religion is more important than the truth. More important than love, more sacred than a human life. In truth, nothing is more important than a single human life.

MYSTICAL NOT RELIGIOUS

To help avoid this trap, the 'Way Within' goes one better than pointing. Instead of merely alluding to the truth it gets you to point at the truth with your own finger and then it helps you to look directly where your finger is pointing. After that first glimpse, it's about taking the time to fully experience what you see. Nothing else is required. You will learn to see without anything added!

A priest tells you what he's been told, a scholar reads, learns and knows nothing, and the faithful listen but are not set free. This is religion. The seer, isn't concerned with listening to words, or studying books and has no truck with faith. The seer is open to the truth, she looks past the finger and has direct experience of 'what-is.' This is mysticism. The seeing mystic has direct experience of God not second-hand platitudes or false sacrament.

The peace, happiness and connectedness that the 'Way Within' helps you to find, will be available to you for the rest of your life. It will always be available, never more than a moment away.

Peace, happiness and connectedness don't require years of study. They don't need rigorous discipline or any special skills or talents.

They are available to all and they're available right now. There is no need to have anything explained or to have an intermediary make it available.

Even for the seasoned seer, there will be times when peace, happiness and connectedness will be replaced by the illusion of fear, sadness and separation. However, in time, like all seers, you will see through the illusion and all will be ok.

In time, you will see through the illusions quicker and dwell in unawareness for shorter spells. In time, you will be able to bring the light of awareness down on life's illusions and all will be peace, happiness and connectedness. All will be revealed for what it 'is', not seen as it 'is not'.

A BETTER PLAN

The 'Way Within' offers you a better plan. It offers a simple, obvious and an easy plan. In a nutshell, we're going to look for our happiness where it is, where it always was and where it always will be.

For this plan to work, we must leave the ego's plan behind. If we don't leave the ego's plan behind, our purpose will be divided between the pursuit of the 'Way Within' and the execution of the ego's plan which is of course the 'Way Without'. The results of a split mind will always be divided and confused.

The end of your search is at hand, or more accurately, nearer than your hand and closer than your breath. The answer, the 'world view' that you've been seeking is so obvious. It's so obvious, that we have all missed it. We've all had a lifetime of missing it!

THE END OF ALL SEEKING

The end of seeking only needs us to redirect our attention for a moment. Once you see the truth, you will never fully lose it again. Blessed by the truth, you won't have to look for anything else ever again.

All's well and all things are well.

Seeking is always a search for what 'is not', seekers are looking for something other than what 'is'.

The end of seeking comes when you embrace what 'is'. Seeking ends when we stop looking for what 'is not', it ends when you stop wanting what 'is' to be other than it 'is'. When you see what 'is' and accept it, then you are found.

All's well, all things are well and suddenly you are well too.

What is found is your true nature and with it you will find peace, harmony and happiness.

THE NATURE OF THE JOURNEY

One of the characteristics of your journey is that in the early stages your grasp of the truth can be fleeting. At first glimpse, the truth will probably be dazzling, and you'll doubt how things could ever be the same again. Gradually though the light will fade as you become acclimatized to the change. It fades as the truth becomes your new normal and the day to day demands of life re-assert control over your attention.

The difference though, is that you have experienced the truth and it never really leaves you again. However, you'll find that awareness does become obscured by all the noise of life.

Initially, there will likely be profound moments of wakefulness followed by longer periods of unawareness as you drift back into your old sleep walk.

However, once you have experienced yourself from zero dis-tance you'll realize that all the peace you've longed for is never more than a thought away. It's this knowledge that moves the balance of life. Increasingly, your life will be lived in the light of awareness and your slumbers will be fewer and shorter. In time, awareness will even permeate your periods of unawareness. You will be aware of your slumbers and raise yourself from your bed when the moment requires it.

As you embrace the 'Way Within' you stop pretending to be something you are not. You'll increasingly drop the need to make up for other people's short comings. You'll stop covering for people's perceived failings. You'll see directly through people's 'faults' to the perfection that is their truth. With acceptance, you'll cease to want things to be other than they are. Finally, you'll merge with the stream of life and move with its ebbs and flows and all will be well, and all things will be well.

HOW LONG DO YOU WANT TO MAKE THE PATH?

The great news is that the path to peace, happiness and clarity is exactly the length we choose to make it. We can spend a life time, indeed many lifetimes, and still not get there. Alternatively, we can have it all this very instant and awaken to our life.

If you want to leave seeking behind and become a seer, then read on. This book is in front of you to help you to look, see and make your own way. It's here so you can find what you really are. It turns out you have an open mind, sometimes though your mind is a little cluttered by all the stuff that stuck to you on the journey to here. None of that stuff is real, none of it takes more than a moment to look past. So, why should you spend a life time becoming what you already are, which is open and loving.

Another way that the 'Way Within' is a direct path lies in the fact that you don't have to de-clutter to achieve the transformation. After transformation with the 'Way Within' you will still have clutter. You will still think insane thoughts and feel the highs and lows of life. However, with awareness nothing can impair your sight of the truth.

Better I think to find peace and happiness here and now rather than waiting until you free yourself of all the clutter. If you try to do that the reality is that you'll likely end up waiting for your deathbed to find eternal peace.

THE LIGHT OF AWARENESS

You don't have to change a thing, not a single thing! All you need to do is bring each trouble into the light of awareness. Once bathed in the aware light, your troubles will dissolve without as much as a finger having to be raised. Trust me, in the light of awareness your troubles will drop away, leaving you free.

Once in the light of awareness troubles disappear leaving the truth. Troubles are just illusions, shadows cast by our thoughts. Like all shadows, they need the light so that they can be seen. Just like shadows illusions can't survive direct exposure to the light.

You can probably sense why a direct path is preferable and effective. It's paradoxical when you think about indirect paths because the very thing they need to progress is only found at the end of the path. This is the beauty and irony of the direct path. With awareness, you can dissolve all the issues of your old life. Ironically, once you embrace your true nature, you really don't have to dissolve your issues as none of them perturb you anymore.

POINTING AT AWARENESS

POINTING OUT WHO AM I

THE SIMPLE EXERCISE I'm about to share with you is based directly on Douglas Harding's simple pointing experiment. This technique has brought me more directly and with greater speed to awareness than any other technique or practice I have yet to hear of. However, that's just me, it's different for everyone.

Unlike many of the things I've read about awareness or enlightenment, Douglas Harding's experiments don't set forth any beliefs, theories, explanations or concepts. Douglas just offers you an opportunity to redirect your attention so that you can experience yourself as you truly are at center. If you take the opportunity, then when you look from zero distance you find yourself as open capacity for life. This exercise is an opportunity to look and take in what you see, notice what you don't see and strive not to be misdirected by what you think.

As we discussed earlier, all down the ages the central question posed by mystics and held by many as the key to enlightenment was "Who am I?" The answer can never be expressed in words, it can only be known, it can never be said. The pointing exercise and Harding's other exercises are an answer to this mystical question. In effect, they will help you to have direct experience and first-person knowledge of "Who I am."

THE POINTING EXERCISE

The Pointing exercise can be done anywhere, anytime and with anyone, in a group or on your own. Personally, I find it best to start the pointing exercise in a relaxed state and from a stationary position. The procedure is as follows.

With your preferred hand point at a distant object or feature. I like to form a fist with my index finger pointing and my thumb resting on my second finger. The exact way you point doesn't matter though I think it's best to do whatever is natural and comfortable. The distance between you and what you point to doesn't matter, it could be across the room, across a valley or across the universe.

I normally start by pointing whatever is opposite me, so right now I'm pointing at the wall opposite. Take a moment to note what you see, for example the objects color, texture and its position relative yourself. Consider the other senses, its smell and sounds and how does it feel to you. Is it part of you or separate?

Figure 4 - Finger pointing at a distant object

Keeping your finger pointing directly at the object and wait for a few moments. Reflect on whatever is being pointed at before moving your finger, so that you're now pointing at the ground in front of you. Again, take a moment to take in the floor. Consider its color, distance, texture, density, feeling and your relationship with it.

Figure 5 - Pointing at the floor

Now point at your foot, any foot it doesn't matter which. While pointing at your foot focus your attention on to the foot in question and take note of what you see, maybe a shoe or sock, note the texture, color and how this foot feels different from the floor you were considering a couple of moments before. Are you separate from your foot, are you inside the foot is the foot inside of you? How is the sensation of your foot different from the perception of the floor or the impression of the object you pointed at?

Figure 6 - Pointing at foot

After a few moments reflection move your finger so it's pointing at your knee. Likewise, let your attention flow to your knee. Again, take note of your knee's shape, color, texture, and its distance from you. Reflect for a moment on these things and how it feels. Is it an object, is it separate from you, are you inside that knee or is it inside of you?

Figure 7 - Pointing at knee

Next rotate your finger up your body so that your hand is pointing directly at your torso. It doesn't matter exactly where on your torso, your naval, diaphragm or your chest are all just fine. Again, follow with your attention to where your finger is pointing. Take in the texture, color and sensations that you find when you follow where your fingers lead.

Figure 8 - Pointing at chest

Finally, and most importantly rotate your finger again so that now it's pointing directly at your face. I find about 6 inches is a good distance. Now look where your finger is pointing. Literally direct your attention away from the pointing finger to the place it's pointing at. Take your time and look at the place, be aware of the place you are looking out from. It's not the hand that you can see from there, instead you are focusing on the place you are seeing from.

Figure 9 - Pointing at center

WHAT IS SEEN AT CENTER?

What can you see? You can see a hovering digit, sure and doubtless some background beyond, but keep your attention on where the finger is pointing at. Do you see any color or structures there? Do you see your face or any signs of a head?

I can see my finger and I'm vaguely aware of the background behind and I can see arms extending from my pointing hand and disappearing into the void. It's not just arms that disappear into this void. My little legs and torso extend up and disappear into this void just below my neck line.

Figure 10 - Pointing arm disappears into the void at my center

For me now, I am aware of the space at my center. I'm aware of the capacity in me for all, the capacity that I look out from and which takes everything in. The space itself is transparent, it has no color and no shape. The space is a blank canvas for whatever comes its way. It accepts all and knows no bounds.

At my center, it appears that I am this spacious capacity, when I take a moment to observe this space, I sense its openness, and know my true nature as clarity and openness. As the capacity, I don't judge, I just accept everything. As spacious capacity, I'm perfectly at peace with everything that comes my way, accepting all, loving all. As capacity for life I'm free of all the ideas, beliefs and opinions that have ruled my life for so long. They are not part of who I am at zero-distance. At zero-distance I am aware-space with capacity for all.

What I can't see is my head, where I've always thought my head was is just this big space. No eyes are seen but one single view is revealed. I'm looking out of the window and the image of a moment back is gone, no trace of it remains as its place has been taken by a new vista.

My face is not here for me because it's there for you. But more on that later!

KEEP LOOKING FOR YOURSELF

Keep looking, don't make this pointing exercise a one-off curiosity or worse something you read about. Keep repeating the exercise and take the time to look carefully at this place, the space. Notice also the place that you are looking out from. You are looking out from the place you are observing. This is a taste of awareness of awareness, the knowing of awareness. This is your first taste of reality. This is the first inkling of all there ever is.

Initially, try to make time every day, and ideally several times a day, to do the pointing exercise. Don't just do the exercise, dwell in that place you find at your center. Linger in the space that you can see all from and in which all appears. Get to know it, feel at home.

Keep curious. Don't revert to your old assumption that you know who and what you are. Keep looking so you can see what you are at zero distance. Pretty much all your life you have been conditioned to believe that you are a person, you are Jamie, John or Jose. But look again, is that what you see at zero distance? Is there a person at your center or is there, as I see, nothing? I see that I am a 'no-thing'. I'm just this spacious capacity for the world?

Don't listen to me, don't dwell on my words, and don't over think it. Look for yourself. What are you? Are you a person or are you just capacity?

Keep looking at the place where others see your face, let it fill with whatever comes along. Look at the things that you are seeing. Is there a distinction between the objects and the awareness of them? The space as I look is bubbling with sounds, objects and sensations, but my experience is that I can't find anything that separates the space or awareness from the things it contains. I find that I am both the spacious capacity and the objects it contains.

WHAT DOES THIS MEAN?

What this all hints at is oneness. No one is outside you, everyone is inside, no one is separate.

When you come to your center you experience the same capacity for all that I do. This capacity is not your capacity, it is just the capacity for all. It is the same capacity for all of us, the exact same capacity, not lots of facsimiles it is the exact same space.

When you dwell on this and feel the universality of the capacity at our center, this awareness starts to change your relationship to everyone. You see me as part of you, nothing I do is separate from you, nothing that happens to me is not happening to you.

DIVINE CENTER

How can you do anything in this awareness to harm me, how can you feel anything but love? How can you ever feel alone again? Everything is in you, there is nothing that you are not. This can be an end too. An end to all thoughts of poverty. You're rich if you just accept everything that is given to you and if you stick with it, you'll come to realize that everything is indeed given to you. More on this later!

I've touched on our divine center but as you become aware of this center, your humanity doesn't fall away. At center I'm divine, spacious capacity and all is well. I'm here for you. On the outside I'm vulnerable, I'm a frail man that can easily be wiped out by a bit of bad weather or any number of everyday things. At center, you are just like me, you are the eternal void out of which all arises and for which there can be no death.

DIVINELY HUMAN

This awareness of both divine and human is what Richard Lang calls living a 'two-sided life.' In awareness, we're now looking both inwards and outwards. I'm both divine and human.

As a human, I'm totally dependent on my divine self as source of all, without which I couldn't survive. Conversely, without my humanity my divine self could not express itself. The all-powerful needs our legs to get about, he needs our hands to do things, our voices to communicate, our hearts to feel. The divine needs us to know itself, to love itself. We are the ultimate expression of love, the ultimate knowledge, we are God saying hello I love you to himself. We are God experiencing God. God loving God. The All loving the All.

ONENESS, NOT ONE AND NOT TWO

Behind this Divine Humanity is oneness, but in a paradoxical way it's not one and not two either. Our relationship with the universe, with God is much more like the relationship between the song and the singer, or the dance and the dancer. Don't fall into the trap of thinking that God is the big dancer and you are the little dancer, no, no, no! That one is an easy trap to fall in to. Better to think of it like God is the dancer and we are being danced.

NOT THAT

WORDS AND TERMINOLOGY

Words are a big trap, we treat them as if they are solid, real. However, words just point to what 'is' or in many cases 'what is not'. As I said earlier, I recommend just letting the words flow over you, don't try to know this book through the words. Try to just look where these words are pointing.

Naturally, I know that many of you will want to get a better understanding of the words I'm using here especially some new words or words that are being used in an unusual way. To this end I have pulled together a section that covers "Some Useful Words and Phrases" and you can find this at the back of the book.

However, if you can resist don't even look at these explanations. Instead just let the words you read wash over you and carry you along.

DESCRIBING WHAT IS NOT

When we think about the language we use to talk about enlightenment or to describe awareness the words that are commonly used only talk about what it is not.

The fundamental problem of language is that language in dualistic in nature. It depends on a subject and an object. The subject describes the object, the object has a form and it is this that our words describe.

Awareness and enlightenment and non-dualistic, they have no form and as such can't be described other than by describing what they are not. Hence, we use words like infinite, eternal, indivisible and ineffable.

The reason we struggle is we are so attached to languages power to describe the form of things. Like good students we end up thinking that it's a failure of our power to find the right words or understand what is being described.

In fact, the issue is that language fails when confronted with the non-dual. It fails in the same way that a drawing on a sheet of paper can't accurately represent a three-dimensional object.

DUALITY IS A PROPERTY OF LANGUAGE

The nature of reality is always non-dualistic, there is only one reality, one moment and all things are one. In fact, there are no things as that implies separation there is just this shifting field of awareness.

To know awareness as awareness, we first look within. At first, we have the experience of being a subject that has awareness and within the awareness there are objects. However, as we deepen our practice and observe the space of awareness and explore its qualities we realize that we can find no subject that knows and no objects that are known. There is just the knowing awareness.

Duality it turns out is just a property of language. We talk about a spinning top, however, we can find no spin that is separate from the top, because spin is a state of the top. Likewise, if we contemplate a vibrating guitar string there is no separation between the string and the vibration. There is no vibration without a string, there is however a string without vibration.

The apparent duality is a property of language only. In awareness, there is no separate object that is a spinning top, the top is a modulation of awareness, awareness doesn't so much know the top as it is the top.

A PRACTICAL GUIDE TO AWARENESS JUST FOR YOU

Above all else, this book is a practical guide so that you can experience seeing for yourself. I'm not in the business of explaining what the ineffable is or telling you where to find the truth.

However, the 'Way Within' helps you to find it all for yourself. This book is here to help you to know yourself as you truly are. It's a guide to experience oneness so that you will know it for yourself, which is the only way to the truth. There's no second-hand knowledge when it comes to awareness, you can't take anyone's word for what oneness is. You must know it for yourself.

DON'T MISTAKE THE MAP FOR THE COUNTRY

There's a lovely story Anthony De Mello shares in 'The Song of the Bird'. In Tony's story, an explorer returns from the Amazon, and naturally everyone wants to know all about the Amazon because they've never been. They've heard magical things but have no idea what the Amazon is really like.

The explorer is full of wonder but he's at a total loss to explain what he experienced. There's just not the words that convey the richness of that place. Finally, he hits on the idea of drawing a map so that people can go and experience first-hand what the Amazon is really like.

The problem is that the people take the map and are totally in awe of it. Instead of following the map, they frame it and put it on a wall and then people start coming from far and wide to look at the map in wonder.

I'm saying to you, use this book exactly as the explorer intended people to use his map. Use it like a map, don't put it on the wall or hold onto a single word. Don't merely read this book, look in the direction it's pointing. Go and see for yourself, you'll find exactly what all words fail to describe. You'll come to see the ineffable, the mystery of mysteries that gives birth to all and when the time comes, destroys it again.

In a sense, this book is about redirecting your attention so that you can see what you are and have awareness of what it is that you experience. Speaking personally this was the first big step on my path to peace of mind and the fulfilment of my life's purpose.

The 'Way Within' is about leaving your seeking behind. Beyond that it's about the transformation into a new state of being that, for want of a better label, I call becoming a 'Seer'.

AWAKENING IS JUST A BEGINNING

An essential catalyst of your transformation is letting go. To sustain the transformation, it's important that as we start to let things go we don't form new attachments.

Read this book, look where it points, then let it go. Burn it, give it away, do anything that avoids hanging on to a single word of it.

One thing that surprises people is that awakening into awareness is just the beginning and represents the first of the big steps on your life's path and steps are more manageable if taken one at a time.

I've confined myself within this book to an exploration of seeing, not least because there's a natural order to this journey and seeing is a great way to start your journey home. You'll know you are home when you reach the happiness, peace and the love that your heart seeks. When you reach the happiness, peace and the love that was yours all along.

Finally, I offer a focus on 'seeing' first because you will get lost if you can't see. Seekers have a tendency go nowhere when they have too much to follow or too much to think about all at once. So, for now just focus on and practice 'seeing'.

Read this book. Bring it home. Live it and don't read another book or explore other practices until you have truly embraced 'seeing'. My ambition is that you will read my next book as a seer and through its pages start living as a sage.

CREATION IS YOUR GIFT

Creation has happened. All time is now, all things are available. It's a paradox for me to talk about your role as a co-creator when all is already created, but don't get lost in words, co-creator is what you are and together we will learn about manifesting what 'is' as the will of God not the whim of man. You'll learn to manifest the part of creation necessary so that Gods will is done.

THE PATHLESS PATH

THE ESSENCE

THERE ARE INFINITE paths to enlightenment but the essence of them is always the same, the ingredients are always the same. The difference is how they come together. How the path comes together is unique to each of us. How you experience this process depends on where you are now, what you've learnt, what you believe and the interplay of your innate qualities and talents.

PATHS AND WAYS

There are many *ways* that you can take to get home but there is only one *path* for you. There are Zen ways, Sufi ways, Buddhist ways, Christian ways, Headless ways, Atheist ways, in fact there's all sorts of ways.

Often people talk about the process of awakening as a journey. Unfortunately, analogies that use journeys can lead to confusion as this is no regular journey. Despite the risk of confusion, I'm going to talk about a journey. I'm going to encourage you to think of the 'Way' as 'how' to get to your destination. In exactly the way that you can go by train, or boat, car, etc.

Whereas, the path is not how you get somewhere. The path is

both the route you take and the stuff that you must take with you on the journey, including the clothes you're wearing. Your path is made up of what you've accumulated in your life and the way is how you free yourself of it all.

In my analogy, you can go lots of ways home, but you always have the same stuff to carry. You can go by train, bus, walk, run or skip and you can go the short cut or the scenic route but regardless of your route or the method of travel you start with the same old stuff you've got to lose along the way.

The stuff you have reflects what you've been doing in your life up to the moment when you start the return leg of your journey. This is the baggage you've picked up along the way. This is the stuff you must shed if you're going to live a life of peace and happiness. There's no strict sequence that needs to be observed as you let go. You just need to drop the things you are attached to!

You could say that your path is made up of the baggage you have picked up through your lifetime, and it is this baggage that the 'way' you follow seeks to free you from.

It's easy, with this analogy, to see how your path is always unique as no one else is ready to set off with the same baggage as you have right now! Clearly, there are lots of ways you can take that will strip you of your baggage. However, be warned, there are many ways that are not good at shedding baggage and most ways will have you picking a whole new load of baggage to pile on top of what you already have!

So, you could say that the way is less like a car or bus and more like a waste basket!

OTHER PEOPLE'S JOURNEY

Just as no one can tell you about your path or know which way is right for you, you can't know someone else's path.

You can observe what's showing up in their lives right now. From your perspective, what shows up in someone else's life is none of your business. What shows up in someone else's life has no meaning to you and if you start to think it does then you are judging them. Judging other people is only ever a movement away from the truth.

You can share your way, and even what you know of paths and

ways but don't get attached to your way or think it's in any way better than any other way. Be very careful with the advice you offer, point but never tell. Be there for people, have compassion, be humble in the face of your total ignorance, never judge. Instead of judging be love.

To move forwards, the person you are dealing with needs to first step back. Then by observing what's showing up in their own life they can figure out what their next step. They will see what needs to be dropped. Personal observation and not your judgement of them is what they need.

AN ENLIGHTENED LIFE

In simple terms, the elements of the enlightened life are: seeing, loving and being. The purpose of your journey is to embrace these aspects of yourself and to bring them to the fore.

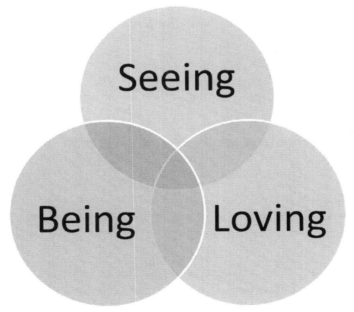

Figure 1 - Seeing, Being and Loving

Ultimately the 'Way Within' is not a way at all, at least it's not a way to do anything. The 'Way Within' is about taking your path and then letting go of all things that stop you from seeing, being and loving. These are the things that now make up you path! It's more a way of not doing, a 'No-way' way.

This letting go is very gentle, it doesn't require you to change a thought or expunge ideas. You just need to be aware of your thoughts and let them be.

The uniqueness of our path is a product of the simple fact that we have all lived different lives. We have different genes, different things to let go of and have different talents to help us on our way. Our talents have a big impact on our choice of 'way' and the rate at which we can let go.

You can't let go of my stuff, letting go of my stuff will do you no good at all, which is why you can't follow my path and why no one else can tell you the right path for you.

However, all is not lost. I'm sharing the 'Way Within' with you so that you can try it out and see if it works for you.

Knowing the difference between ways and paths makes it much easier to find a way that does work for you. I can help you to understand your own path for yourself; this seeing is independent of all ways.

Trust me, it will be hard to avoid the things that are keeping you from seeing, loving and being. They announce themselves all the time without the slightest subtlety and you have an arsenal of senses for detecting them! Be assured your path will be revealed!

STEPWISE ENLIGHTENMENT

The 'Way Within' books focus on 'seeing' first, then on 'being' and 'loving', and finally they bring you to 'oneness'. Seeing, being, loving and oneness are the focus of the next book. The books approach these aspects of the way in sequence making the lessons easier to absorb and ushering you along your personal path of awareness in gentle steps. However, each book must touch on all of them as they're intrinsic to the way, which is, after all, only about removing those things that separate you from seeing, loving, being and oneness.

There's more to this way than just seeing, being and loving. There is also your purpose and how to achieve this as co-creator of what 'is'.

Although the books present this as steps, and you can tackle seeing, being and loving one at a time, oneness is only be lived when it all comes together.

A REVEALING PARADOX OF NIRVANA

One paradox of Nirvana, or Enlightenment is that you can't get half way there. You are either there or you're not, you're either enlightened or you're not, you're in Nirvana or you're not.

In my experience, you will probably experience enlightenment, and then at other times you'll experience its absence, you will never experience being a bit enlightened. Though many of us experience an afterglow of lingering bliss that is enlightenments residue.

We also experience the residue of our old lingering feelings of being a separate mind long after we recognize our true nature.

As you progress with the 'Way Within', you will get many benefits. Benefits like peace of mind, bliss, wishes fulfilled and miracles a plenty. Be warned. Do not mistake these for enlightenment; they are beautiful, delicious and if you are not watchful they are dangerously distracting.

I also flag the all or nothing quality because the paradox gives a sense of the journey in front of you. Pre-warned is pre-armed! So, don't be disappointed, and don't be too hard on yourself when you slip back into old habits and unawareness swallows you up again. Don't be surprised when you continue to feel separate, this is totally normal and should be expected!

A STRANGE KIND OF A JOURNEY

What sort of journey can you take where you can start, you can finish but you can never be part way there?

In a way the answer is obvious, it can only be a journey of no distance. We've decided to go back to a home we never left, we've decided to be present in a present that always is. The difference is that this time we are going to be there, or rather be here, in awareness!

This paradox also frames a warning. There are ways that seem to be going in the right direction but in the end, they don't go all the way. These are alluring stepping stones which will take you to the middle of the stream and then just leave you stranded!

The journey of no distance is a way of wholeness that will bring you to oneness with all that life is.

NO STEPS REQUIRED

So, if the 'Way Within' is a journey of no distance, then what you have always wanted is right here, right now. You don't have to go somewhere else, you don't need to know anything else and you don't have to wait another second to reach your goal. It's no coincidence that I keep talking about getting home.

YOUR PATH IS REVEALED

As you progress through life it provides you with endless opportunities to let go of all the things that are keeping you from seeing, being and loving. In fact, life keeps throwing these things right in front of you.

Everything you do that doesn't lead to peace, love and happiness, reveals what is keeping you from the truth. In a way, all you should do is listen quietly and all will be revealed. I say all you should do. However, listening quietly is a major challenge for most of us.

Part of this is about following the bliss. However, when you don't feel blissful it's a good time to practice your observation skills. Don't do anything, but watch yourself, what's in front of you, what's annoying you, what's making your scared, what's causing that tightness inside you.

This is your work! There's nothing wrong with what's in front of you but there's plenty that's wrong about your thinking in relation to what's before you. You don't have to stop thinking, far from it, you just need to be aware. More on this later!

THE JOURNEY METAPHORE REVISTED

The direct path is about knowing that you are the naked truth. You're not the things that you cling to. It's all the clinging that stops you finding peace and your own perfection. In awareness, you don't just lose your baggage, you release the bits that need to be dropped off. In awareness, you realize that your path is about noticing when it's time to drop the next bit off.

Paradoxically, you don't need to drop anything because you know your truth. However, in awareness each piece drops away in gentleness and in its own good time. You kiss it all goodbye with gracious gratitude. No effort required!

THE 'WAY WITHIN' IS TRULY OPEN TO ALL

The 'Way Within' unlike many ways, doesn't bring any ideas or require you to adopt a new world-view, although a bright new view of the world is an inevitable consequence of adopting it. There's nothing to learn, no language to master, no sacrament and no rituals to follow. However, the exercises that we will discuss later are transformational in helping you to see for yourself.

One of the most striking things about the 'Way Within' is that it complements all other ways. The 'Way Within' is truly open to all faiths, all backgrounds, and all people rich, poor, smart or simple.

HEART OF THE GREAT TRADITIONS

When we examine the mystical roots of all the world's great religions, we find a consistent message about our nature and our purpose in life. We find at the heart and mystical beginnings of Hinduism, Buddhism, Taoism, Judaism and Christianity the belief that we are all part of one central reality; this insight has many names, but Awareness works best for me. Furthermore, all the mystical traditions point towards a return to our source, a return to our center, they promote a coming home to oneself, and they suggest we look inside and be what we are.

The 'Way Within' strips away all the baggage that the great traditions have picked up down the ages and gives you the tools to come home and be yourself. It brings you back to the home you never really left and leaves you to know that place for the first time.

Don't be too hard on yourself when you get a little lost on the way. Getting lost is an important part of your path, just like the traditions you have much baggage to shed, it's probable that your stuff is the same stuff that shrouds the truth from all religious devotees.

ALCHEMY

You are the alchemist of your own transformation. Only you can turn your fear, worry, anger and hatred into love, openness, kindness and awareness.

Your path is none of my business. I can never know what's going to be on it, I can't tell you what to do or even what not to do. In this way, I'm not a teacher and although I talk about a way, be careful because my words can be a problem. It's important you don't make too much of the words, don't get stuck with them. Instead, look where the words are pointing and go and discover that place for yourself. Look at what's in front of you and watch it transform into love, peace and happiness.

The ways are many, but the path is one. I can't open your eyes to the one that is many, only you can open your own eyes and see what is. You are the alchemist not me. I'm just a way-shower, a sign post; all the magic is down to you. You are the only one that can turn the lead in your life into gold. That is your miracle to perform, this is your gift.

You are the Alchemist!

THREE RULES OF TRANSFORMATION

If you are serious about making this journey home, then I ask only three things:

1. Do the exercises.
2. Go with what you experience, not what you already know.
3. Use what you discover.

These three rules are all I ask of you!

RULE 1 – DO THE EXERCISES

This rule is the cornerstone. The truth is that you will get nothing from just reading this book. You must do each exercise. You must stop and let the miracle happen inside you. This takes time and a little effort on your part. No brainer really!

I know from personal experience what happens if you just read. I've read so many books and maybe because I was always on a train or somewhere similar I rarely stopped to put the lessons into practice. In a sense, I was just a voyeur. My non-participation wasn't restricted to books either. I watched YouTube videos listened to podcasts, and although the books, videos and podcasts often resonated with me there was no transformation for me as a viewer or listener.

The transformation came for me when I went to a workshop. It occurred when I threw myself into gaining first-person experience as opposed to stuffing my head with more second-hand knowledge.

I think it's quite common for us seekers to miss Rule 1 (Do the exercises) as we're so eager to devour ever more information. We rip through books and before we can really take in what's just been read and apply it, we're already onto the next book and all the goodness is lost.

This illustrates another problem. What we are looking for is here and now, right under our noses. As seekers, we read a book or go to a workshop, we bring knowledge into the here and now only to look right past it to something else out there at the end of another avenue that will be ours at another time, indeed any time other than now.

Let's be clear, you'll get nothing from just reading the exercises. Reading the exercises without trying them is worse than doing nothing because you'll be wasting your time. Time is precious, once it slips through your fingers it's gone forever.

Do each exercise, and keep with it, repeating often. Better still, join a group or work with friends and share the experience.

RULE 2 – GO WITH WHAT YOU FIND

When you undertake the exercises, try to ignore everything you've been brought up to believe, and instead just take the time to look for yourself. Take the time to notice what you experience. Even if you only manage a minute or two, just take it in. If thoughts bubble into consciousness, try to leave them unattended. Be aware if you judge or pigeon-hole things. Instead of letting your thoughts direct you, try to just let them in unmolested, let them wash over you.

Don't let your thoughts inform you about your experience, let them come and go without taking much notice. Look beyond the thoughts about what you are looking at to what is seen without any thoughts.

I'm asking you to start from nothing and trust your own feelings. Be prepared to discover that you are more blessed than you could ever have imagined.

The experience of your true nature is non-verbal and non-judg-mental. Thoughts and beliefs are mostly verbal in nature and engender judgements. Thoughts about what 'is' happen after the actual experience and take you out of the moment if you indulge them. In contrast, observing your thoughts happens in the now and keeps you at peace.

The second rule is a commitment to go with what you find. There will be instructions for each exercise. However, each exercise is really all about you. If you just follow the instructions and if you're open and honest you can't go wrong.

RULE 3 – USE WHAT YOU DISCOVER

This is obvious but often overlooked by seekers. It's like winning the lottery. Just like a lottery winner you'll have a lot in the bank, you might be rich beyond your wildest imagining, but if you don't spend some of it you'll live your life just as it was before. Poor!

The paradox of the 'Way Within' is that you end up squandering this bounty if you don't spend it. You should spend it like it's the last day of the sales. As you awaken, share what you have gained through your awakened actions. Share what you are and through your authenticity, your actions and authenticity show people what they too can be too.

Many seekers get a glimpse of what they are. Indeed, many can tell you what they are in terms of oneness, love and peace but these same people totally fail to be those things in the very next moment. Don't let the moment pass again, be what you are.

Being yourself, being authentic is the most liberating and blissful thing! Don't sweat it if you fail, don't worry if you slip back into old habits, we all do. Instead of worrying about it, let your failure be an alarm clock that wakes you into awareness. Let the little failures wake you up rather than plunging you into self-recrimination and unawareness.

Likewise, don't linger in awe. Don't live a life of contemplation and reflection. When you come to see how you are perfect peace and contended bliss, go out and be the things that you are: be love, be peace and be happiness in the world.

NEW AGE OF ENLIGHTENMENT

Something radical has happened in the last century or so and for the first time in recorded history significant numbers of people all around the world are awakening into awareness. Today the gift of enlightenment is enjoyed by thousands of people all around the world, whereas in the past this gift was bestowed upon one or two divine beings each generation. The process of awareness is accelerating now exactly because more people are aware. With more people, and thanks to the internet, more of us get to spend time with awakened folk. More of us get inspired by the new illuminati through their work and achievements.

The opportunity is here for you to follow where these enlightened folks are pointing, but again (you probably guessed it), be careful not to follow in their footsteps.

You will find your path by following your own innate spiritual sense. The good news is that we all have this innate sense and the process of awakening is accessible to all. This process was never about learning things it's simply about awakening to life. Make the 'Way Within' your wake-up call. Make the exercises your daily spiritual coffee.

THE WAY WITHIN IS YOUR PLAN Z

To give some context, I sometimes talk about the 'Way Within' as my Plan Z. This new plan, this Plan Z is a paradox. On the one hand it's the simplest plan, on the other hand it's the most radical plan and requires you to turn the world upside down and inside out.

I don't call it Plan B because most of you have already tried Plan B. Plan B is where you drop the material search and replace it with a spiritual search. Some of you have tried Plan C, where you try to change the way you think about the world. You've probably dabbled with Plan D, where you try to change yourself or Plan E where you change what you do. I don't like Plan F where you must rid yourself of all karma, all the time heaping up more behind you as you go. Like many plans, Plan F is fraught with danger not least of which is mental and physical exhaustion, which ironically is the only hope you have of making a break through. Plan G, is a personal favorite of mine, where you hide from reality by looking for the truth in scholarly works. All you must do is master this text, but each text leads to a dozen more, each one taking you further from reality.

One of the most dangerous plans, Plan H is the one where you try to take the ego on. Don't take on the ego, for he's a cunning beast and he'll drag you down to his level where he is the master. Giving your ego attention just feeds him, better to stand back, leave him be. Besides, he can't make an appearance in the now.

If you are prone to dabble with Plan H remember Ramana Maharishi's words: "Never mind the mind... There is no mind to control if you realize the self... You have ignored what is real and are holding on to the mind which is unreal".

I could go on and on, but I think my point is clear and I bet there are many, many, other plans and variations that I've not mentioned that you've fallen foul of.

If you're honest, you'll have to admit that you've been trying some pretty crazy plans whether conscious of what you were doing or not. They're all versions of the ego's plan and none of them work. The plan I'm offering you is nature's plan, the universe's plan, it's the last plan and it brings the end of all seeking. It's the plan with nothing added.

It's the final plan. It's the last thing you'll do because once it's completed there will be no more doing, just being and things will be done. Don't panic, you're not going to get home only to drop dead. No, this is about waking up from your slumbers and living life to the full.

The great irony of the search is that in the end what you are looking for is right here, right now, exactly where you are. The 'Way Within' takes you back to where you started, only this time you will really know this place for the first time.

NOT A THERAPEUTIC OR SPIRITUAL PATH

There are many spiritual paths and therapeutic practices that aim to address the issues in your life and fix them. The 'Way Within' is not a therapy or a spiritual path. Paraphrasing from Chang Chen Chi's, 'The practice of Zen', the 'Way Within' overlooks the many layers of your mind and instead it aims to penetrate to your minds core because once this core is grasped all else becomes crystal clear and relatively insignificant.

The 'Way Within' is here to direct your focus from an eccentric, or if you prefer ego-centric view of the world to what I'll be calling a zero-centric view. The 'Way Within' will redirect you from seeing the world as you believe 'you are' to seeing the world as 'it is'. The

'Way Within' is about seeing from that place of peace that is at the heart of us all. It is about seeing the world from zero distance, not through the filters we add to it. In effect, it's about seeing the world without anything added. Take the 'Way Within' and you'll abandon your ego-centricity, with all its fear and suffering. You'll become zero-centric from where you'll find liberation from all suffering. From here, and here only, you can live a life of peace, happiness and meaningful purpose.

MY JOURNEY HOME

MY EARLY LIFE'S PATERN

FOR ALMOST HALF a century my life followed a familiar pattern of pain, longing and hope. There were fleeting moments of euphoria followed by yet more dull longings. Don't get me wrong, I was happy, I was successful, and I was blessed with good health. I had a wonderful family and friends who loved me, yet something was missing. There was a void, call it an emptiness, and nothing I did or acquired or even experienced could take away my need to fill this void.

THE MAN OF SUBSTANCE

As a young adult, I was totally committed to being something in the world. I was obsessed with securing possessions, harvesting experiences and creating an impression on other people. All my efforts to improve myself were driven by the desire to be a bigger something in the world and to have more stuff and engage myself in ever richer experiences.

THE SPIRITUAL SEEKER

One sunny morning in my thirties I woke up to the fact that something was wrong and because of this insight I shifted my longing from material stuff towards a spiritual path. This shift didn't happen overnight. I'd been interested in self-improvement and philosophy ever since I was a teenager. However, what did change was that I realized that the answer wasn't more stuff or status. From this point forwards, my efforts to improve myself were no longer about getting more stuff or more status.

After more years of seeking, and now into my forties, I'd developed quite a deep knowledge and an extensive tool-kit of spiritual practices. I knew about projection, the ego, attachment, detachment, forgiving, judgement, surrender, blessings, gratitude, observation, openness, oneness, karma, non-duality, the holy instant, miracles and so much more. However, despite all this, somehow, I'd just swapped a fruitless path for an endless one. I had knowledge but wasn't very wise!

FAILURE OF THE SEEKER

I was totally ridiculous. I'd ditched the 'big' me, that had been my life's work, for a 'higher' me that was a whole new life's work. I'd swapped one fiction for another, one ego for another, one side of the coin for the other. I'd become a spiritual person, a seeker. My ego had swapped its little devil horns for a golden halo. The great irony was that it was this new seeking that was now keeping me from the truth.

I'm a very lucky man because long before it was too late, long before another lifetime slipped through my fingers, I glimpsed what was going on. Very slowly I started to see through this 'higher me' instead of seeing the world with the 'higher me'. I could see that my seeking was acting like a lens that was obscuring and distorting the truth, a lens that was contorting my perception of the world at large.

I'd finally seen that the spiritual and the material were just different aspects of a greater whole. I realized that whether worldly or spiritual, it was all just seeking. It was all directed towards a future 'me' that was never going to happen. It was all distracting me from the 'now' and from 'this'.

This was a time of revelations for me, they came fast and furious and in their wake, all my seeking fell away. In fact, pretty much everything fell away. I fell away and I was left with peace, truth and understanding and a few concerned friends and relatives.

People have asked me how the revelations came about, what they really mean is how do I have similar revelations. However, there is no 'how' beyond the truth, and that when you start to see clearly, when you see what 'is', when you stop seeing what you believe or think, then you are left with the truth and there is no greater revelation than the simple undiluted knowing of what 'is'. There's no greater revelation than the falling leaf of fall, or the rising sun of dawn, or by the evident love that is masked by the delinquent's actions.

THINKING ME, CREATOR AND HOST

I'd started out by thinking that my thoughts arose from what was happening. Then I'd believed that my thoughts projected my perception of things onto the world. I thought that I created the world in my own image. Finally, I realized that there were no things in the world, it was all in me. I saw that I was not only the creator. I was the container or host of all things too.

I'd realized that while there was a sense of a 'me' seeking then I'd always be separate. I realized that the container was not in this body I'd been thinking of as 'me'. The container was awareness and it contained only awareness and I was that.

Being separate is an insurmountable obstacle when what you are longing for, is to be whole. I wanted oneness.

Like so many of us seekers, I'd believed in oneness, I'd believed in its reality. However, I had been blind to it because I was sheltering in my separateness. I was looking for oneness for 'me.' As if it was something that I can get tomorrow, something I can have. How crazy is that, as if I can have oneness and you can't.

The irony, the beauty, the vanity of it all makes me laugh at myself for my many inevitable, yet necessary blunders. Be gentle on yourself, as I am on me.

GOD KNOWING GOD

It's interesting because, as we set off towards oneness, as we go looking for oneness, what we find first is our separateness.

This separation is the opposite of the state we experienced before we were born. I think this points to why God created us with this sense of separateness. It points to why we exist, seemingly, apart from the universe.

We are created separate, longing to know wholeness. Whereas God was and is everything, God is whole. However, before man came into being, the one thing God couldn't do was to know himself. She couldn't marvel at herself because she had no perspective. God had created a universe of wonder. She could see everything, know everything, do everything, and be everything. The one thing that she was denied was to experience herself because she lacked a point of view. She was whole, all powerful and then she imagined separation. She saw that separation gave her the one thing that she didn't have; a mirror.

Hence, she created us separate, and now the twist is that we long for wholeness.

Of course, I don't know any of this, this is just the creation myth that I like to foster. The myth that God created us separate so that she could know herself. In other words, we are just God knowing herself. We are God looking at her awesomeness and reflecting "wow this is great!"

When we talk, it's God talking to God. When I see you, it's God seeing God!

I love this world view and when I chance to meet with someone else that has this God awareness it's a magical moment.

GOD AWARENESS DIVINE GRATITUDE

From 'zero-distance' I create the universe. Every event, all of history happened for this moment. The whole universe just now conspired to bring me a tea on the 16:43 to Edinburgh, the stewardess is a goddess and she exists for me, she is me. She's not a figure moving through the theatre of my mind or perception. No, I am her. I love her so much and she smiles because she sees it in my eyes.

I chuckle to myself in the knowledge that Hannibal had to cross the Alps and wage war for 18 years in Italy, Caesar had to cross the Rubicon and Pompey had to wage world war. Christ had to be crucified, disease had to be overcome, lovers loved, the guilty hanged, seamen lost at sea; just so that I can have this cup of tea. Suddenly it tastes divine and I know gratitude.

THE FALL

Coming back to my journey, I wish I could say I did this or I did that to bring about my release from seeking, but the truth is, that I just came to a point where it all just dropped away. I didn't try to do anything, I just stopped. I just let go. It was the irresistible weight of first-person experience and the effect of the only true knowledge there is. The knowing of experience.

I moved from thinking that I know nothing, or put another way, I moved from the idea of knowing nothing and arrived at the first-person wisdom of knowing nothing, and with this knowing came such freedom, such total liberation.

I woke from the dream of the separate, to the understanding that I was never separate, and I can never be separate again. Of course, I would often feel separate, but I would never be separate; more on this subtle point later! I woke and found that the search of a life time was the search for home. As I woke I realized that I'd never left home, yet now I was back home.

THE TRAP OF THE ENLIGHTENED

I won't say that I became enlightened as any such statement is an error and misleading. There was a long time preceding my fall, where I wanted to be enlightened, and times when I wondered if I was enlightened, but now I see that in this way enlightenment is a perilous trap. The very thought of me becoming enlightened reveals that I was still thinking of a separate me, a me getting enlightenment, a separate thinking self. This separate thinking self was one of the last things to fall away. This lingering sense of superiority, the sense that I can have something that you can't and that I can get something, the belief that I can get anything for me.

Take a moment. Are you seeking enlightenment? Do you want to get it?

Enlightenment can't happen to me or you, it can't be had. It's a lovely illusion and one that the ego makes its own. It was first-person experience that released me from this trap and you will find awakening comes gracefully to you when you look and see and embrace the life that is. It comes when you relax and stop fighting life and learn to love 'this' as it is with nothing added. It comes when you learn to be gentle on yourself and with others. It's revealed when you stop seeking and start seeing.

I didn't stop having negative thoughts, feelings, emotions or stupid ideas but I did stop being these thoughts. Suddenly, I wasn't stupid, depressed or happy. Stupid, depressed or happy, was just how I felt from moment to moment. Generally, I didn't get caught by these thoughts or feelings. These tricksters stopped living me and if they did snag me, the trap rarely lasted more than a few moments before I could laugh at myself. With laughter and a light touch these thoughts went on their way and I silently, lovingly and patiently watched them.

Don't over concern yourself with any of this. Let it wash over you for now. We'll come back to this with real purpose and the right perspective in the next book. For now, concentrate on seeing. Seeing is a relatively easy first step and an inevitable catalyst for the transformation that follows it.

YOUR JOURNEY HOME

THE GOOD NEWS

WELL, THE GOOD news is that your journey home doesn't have to be as meandering as my trip. You don't have to spend years learning stuff or sitting in contemplation. No, you can take the direct route home. You can have peace, awareness and understanding wherever you are now, and you can have it no matter what is happening. You can live a life of love and bring love to all those you touch.

I'm guessing in any case that you've done all the learning and meandering you need and it's time to be the transformation you're looking for.

This book is not about sharing insights into what enlightenment is or how you can be enlightened. You won't find any secrets and trust me it doesn't require a degree in metaphysics, whatever that is, to get home. Ironically, it does seem that the more sophisticated you are, the harder the way often is. Obviously, it's not that being sophisticated you'll find it harder to grasp. It's that the more sophisticated you are, the more you'll have to let go of. Also, as a sophisticate you'll be so much more attached to all that wonderful stuff you've spent your lifetime learning.

YOUR GUIDE

I'm here to help you discover the truth for yourself. When it comes to the truth, there's no getting away from the fact that you'll have to find it for yourself. I can't reveal the truth to you, no person or book can do that. However, I will try to guide you to experience it for yourself. I will help you find your own way home, and trust me, the personal experience and the knowledge it brings is worth more than all the words ever written about it. You won't want to swap your true home for the grandest of palaces or swap your life for the life that goes with such worldly privilege. No one, once they grasp the truth, wants to swap peace, happiness and right action for fear, insecurity and dis-ease.

Your journey home, like this book, is about how you see the world. Unless you get seeing sorted out you will never break out of the cycle of fear and illusion that keeps you in the dark.

Seeing is one of the sacred keys to a life of peace, happiness and fulfilment. Seeing is the light switch for your life. You can stay in the dark or you can wake up and start living your life. You can keep seeking out there or you can come home and be here and now!

THE VIEW FROM HERE

With seeing comes a marvelous opportunity. With seeing you can experience your experiences. With seeing you can dare to be yourself and view life from where you are, not from where you are not! With seeing you can embrace mindfulness practices.

Your journey is not an eccentric indulgence, it's about being zero-centric, about seeing at zero distance. Your journey home is about being here, where you always are, not over there where you've never been.

The trouble is, that until now you've put all your energy and all your hopes and dreams into the story of 'me'. All your energy is invested into that face over there. Put another way, you've been putting all your energy into the 'me' that's a few centimeters removed from the 'I' at your center. You've put everything into something only to watch it slowly crumble with the passing years.

MAKE THE SHIFT FROM 'ME' TO 'I'

The transformation that I keep referring to is the shift from looking as 'me' to seeing as 'I'. This is about being the aware 'I' that sees 'as-is'. Seeing with nothing added, seeing not through your ego and beliefs, but seeing as you truly are. In other words, it's the shift from seeing the world out there as a reflection of your thoughts, to seeing the world at zero distance without anything obscuring the view. It's about seeing what 'is' without anything added.

It's important to understand that your journey is about knowing the truth of who you are at 'center'. At 'center' and from zero distance you are open, wide open. At 'center' you are spacious capacity for life, without judgements and perfect in all ways.

For most people, these are just more words. The point of this book is to get you to see for yourself and know yourself as you are. The point is for you to experience the intimacy of knowing. The point is to know yourself as an open spacious capacity for all.

YOUR APPEARANCE

Your whole life you've been told stories and facts that convince you that you are something in the world, a person, solid, of a certain height, and weight, and color. It's this story of being something in the world that is the root of all your stress. It's this something that is subject to stress.

In a way, all the stories reflect how people see you. It's also a reflection of how they see themselves and the broader story of the society in which you live. From over there, people are right, that is how you appear. However, how you appear also changes again and again depending on the distance from which you are viewed.

Critical for our purpose, critical for discovering the truth, there is one view, a universal view of you, a view that is quite special and uniquely yours, yet paradoxically the same for all viewers. This universal view is: how you look to yourself from zero-distance.

Don't confuse this universal view with how you look in the mirror, that's how you look from eighteen inches not zero distance. The face which you look at in the mirror is over there. Whereas, here there is no face, just space. This is the view from zero distance, the view from here, this is the view from nowhere.

REGIONAL VIEWS

From three feet, I look like a regular guy. Come closer and your view becomes just the bit of me that's in focus, maybe my face or maybe a hand. Come closer and what do you see? My skin, pores, hairs. Come closer and you'll see the cells that make up my skin. Come closer and you'll see the molecules that make up these cells. Come closer and you can see the atoms, then the sub atomic particles, and beyond which who knows.

Moving away I morph into a building, a town, a country, a planet, a solar system, a galaxy, a universe and again no one really knows where it stops.

The point is how we appear, is a product of our distance from the viewer. Our appearance from moment to moment is always a regional view.

ZERO DISTANCE FROM YOURSELF

The Way Within is about getting a true vision of yourself, swapping the view from over there that other people have of you, for the view from where you are here and now. This view from here, is not how you imagine it to be from over there. It's not a view of you or indeed a view of anything as a thing in the world, it's the experience of yourself as spacious capacity.

This view from center isn't another regional view, it's not merely a matter of appearances from different distances. It is what those regional appearances are appearances of. It's the central reality that gives rise to all the views. It's not what you look like, it's what you are, it's what Buddha was, and it's what Christ was. It's the 'I am, that I am'.

This journey of yours is from the superficial to the profound! The exercises that follow will carry you on this journey, do them and be what you discover you are!

This book is about seeing what you are, the next book deals with being content with what you see and being it to the full, being alive to it all. In this contentment, in this being, you will find your sagehood, but first you must become a seer.

THE JOURNEY TO 'NO STRESS'

Much of our stress in life arises from a reluctance to see for ourselves and our habit of allowing ourselves to be guided by social pressure.

The exercises help you to see that there is no-thing inside of you. The exercises enable you to experience your nothingness. In this way, they help you to know that you have nothing of your own and to know yourself as the nothingness.

With practice, you'll come to see that there is nothing inside of you to be stressed. You'll realize there's nothing of you to be 'got at' by these pesky bodies in the universe that are constantly exerting pressure on each other. You'll see that there's nothing to be stressed, nothing that is stressed, nothing to be pushed and squeezed.

Through the exercises, you'll also come to see that this emptiness of yours has no limits, no boundary beyond which outsiders could lurk bringing undue pressures on you.

Your journey is to know that you are this 'no-thing / all-things' and as such your gift is to enjoy liberation from all stress!

The irony is that the real you, this 'no-thing / all-things' was never capable of stress! The irony is that this 'no-thing / all-things' is no duality, there is no splits in your nature, you are entirely non-dual.

I said at the beginning, that much of our stress comes from a reluctance to see for our self. This sounds like a platitude when you are facing loss, chronic illness, death or disaster. However, as painful as these things are, the truth is that our reluctance to see what 'is', is the source of all stress. I'm not being crass, when you are deep in stress, then this wisdom sounds hollow and idealistic. Another truth then, is that when you are in a world of pain, this becomes your truth. To be frank, it's insulting to suggest that you just need to look. I don't wish to insult you, I love you, and if you are feeling too much pain to face on your own, then it's probable that you need a therapeutic intervention to break you out of your current patterns of thought.

THE STRESS BODY

Stress is a function of the body. The more we live in the body, the more we live for the body. The more we live through the body, the greater our sense of stress.

When you are willing, the 'Way Within' helps you to see through the body, not with it. The 'Way Within' takes you beyond body awareness so that you can know and live as the 'I Am.' To live beyond the body. The 'Way Within' takes you from unawareness to awareness. Unawareness is of the body, it is illusion, and it is finite. Awareness is infinite, it is the truth and you are that.

You are not your body, you are more, and the body doesn't have you. No body no stress. You are not a mind in a body either. You are the spacious capacity of awareness in which all things appear.

The body is another illusion that keeps you from love. Let it go, drop the attachment and the pain will go, the stress will go, the fear will go and Love will flow. Drop the body and it will serve you well, it will allow you to be the Love that you are in the world. Drop the body, and your will, will be done. Hang on to the body and you will be distracted and time will slip through your fingers.

Dropping the body is hard to do when you don't have a viable alternative. The good news is that exercise that follow do more than give you an alternative, they set you free.

EMPTINESS IS REAL

For years, I felt that something was missing. I had a sense of lack. Many of us have this feeling, a feeling of emptiness. There is no lack, there is nothing missing. This feeling is an insight, it's a deep knowing of your truth, a feeling that you mistake for lack. Nothing is our true nature. We are the void from which the miracle of life emerges and into which all things eventually collapse.

GETTING WHAT YOU WANT

What is it that you truly want from life? This is a big question for all seekers and I want you to take a few moments to think about it.

Another question for us all to think about is, "Do we ever really get what we want?"

When what we want does show up in our life it quickly seems inadequate or at least humdrum. My experience has been that what little satisfaction or relief things offer is normally limited and fades quickly.

The 'Way Within' is about finding that which not only satisfies but goes on satisfying. I want you to know that this universal satisfaction exists, it's never remote and it's not hard to find.

THE THREE WANTS

There are three desires or wants:

1. What you think you want.

2. What you really want.

3. What the universe wants.

Douglas Harding calls these the "Three areas of the will" and he shows the relationship between the three wills as a Venn diagram with all types of desire being contained within (3) 'What the Universe wants.'

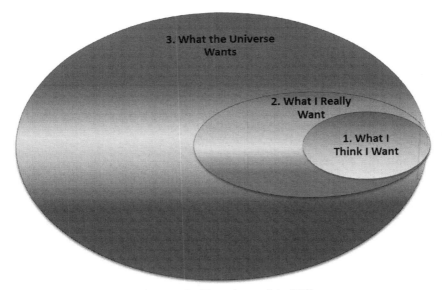

Figure 2 The Three Areas of the Will

There's often a conflict between (1) 'What you think you want' and (2) 'What you really want.' This conflict is mostly hidden from the outside world. Often, we go to lengths to hide this conflict from ourselves too.

This conflict is evident when we are 'faking it till we make it.'

When we act 'as if', we make a big show. We are telling the world that we want the object of our desire while secretly telling ourselves that we already have it. The object can be a thing or role or habit.

This is the game that many people that are keen for self-improvement advocate and follow. However, it's a dangerous route as the associated conflicts will, in time, lead to dis-ease if not nipped in the bud.

There's also a conflict between (1) 'What you think you want' and (3) 'What the universe wants.' This is the conflict between desire and reality. This is where we reject 'what-is' by adding 'what-is-not' to it and then lamenting the present moment's perceived inadequacies.

The 'Way Within' takes away the conflict between these desires, and it reveals that what you want is literally 'what-is.' Through the 'Way Within' you become aligned with (3) 'What the universe wants.'

STRESS AND THE WILL

Any gap between what we think we want and what we really want will result in stress.

Sometimes our hidden motives are baser than those we show to the world, at other times they are nobler. In other words, we make a show of doing things for good reasons, when our true motives are not good but selfish. At other times, we appear to be selfish when we are in fact doing what is good.

It's been said that saints don't know what they are doing is good and heroes don't see themselves as heroic.

Seekers are not generally consciously aware of their motives. However, much of their seeking is driven by the need to be rid of their sense of misalignment between their actions and their true purpose. Once aware of the misalignment of their actions and purpose it becomes a powerful motivation to release us from our sense of dis-ease.

As seekers and having awoken to our limited capacity for satisfaction from worldly achievement, we are now looking for something that not only satisfies, but goes on satisfying. Often, as seekers we sense that by being authentic, we will have peace of mind and the bliss that flows from liberation. This becomes the big search for truth and how to be authentic in our lives.

The beautiful thing is that what we seek is, in the end, just what 'is'.

The seekers journey is a search to find what we really want and then live our lives from there as an alternative to living from what we think we want.

Ironically, the 'Way Within' reveals that we are what the universe really wants. We not only contain the world but 'intend' the world and in time we discover that we really want it all.

It was just a case of 'what you want' getting in between 'what you really want' and 'what the universe wants'. Through the 'Way Within', you learn and finally practice the love of what 'is', and it's this that is satisfying and goes on satisfying forever.

When you embrace this truth, you are happy indeed. When you wholeheartedly choose what 'is' all your stress vanishes.

Choosing what 'is' is no choice at all, it is just the act of love, it arises from a knowing of your true nature as awareness, as the always open capacity for life. Wanting anything other than what 'is', needing anything arises from a sense of separation, it is always thought born. Loving what is, arises from an alignment with, from a knowing of and a 'being' your true nature.

This is the great secret of life. This is your journey.

YOU MUST SEEK FIRST

Be warned. The people around you might not see your seeking in a positive light. They might well think that you are being selfish. They might resent that as you become more aware you stop playing the games people play. They almost certainly won't want to hear the truth as you now see it if it contradicts their world view.

I'm afraid you must be selfish. You must look for the truth and learn to love what is. You must find peace for yourself first, if you are to bring peace to the world at large.

It's a bit like being on a plane that depressurizes, if the oxygen masks fall from the ceiling, you must secure your own mask first before you can help anyone else.

OBJECTIONS

I'm guessing the mere suggestion of embracing 'what-is' brings waves of objections to your mind. The universe is so often cruel, dangerous and painful. How could you love that? How could you advocate that? The bitterest pill is in many ways the notion that you don't merely accept the world and all its ills, you intended it. How could you will it so?

The questions keep coming: What price then for this happiness? Does it have to cost your humanity and your compassion? Do you have to drop your revulsion at the many evils of the world? Would this sort of sacrifice make any bliss you experienced a false bliss, the bliss of an ostrich with his head buried deep in the sand? Is that sort of bliss stress-free? You've probably thought at times that God is cruel, and if not thought it, you've certainly heard it said. However, are you his partner in crime? If you intend it all then surely you are more than some sort of cosmic lackey, you're a major criminal?

Don't worry, these are just thoughts and we all have them. Rest assured, in the light of awareness you will see these as the tricks of the half-light that they are.

THE TRAP OF ACCEPTANCE

Many spiritual ways advocate the practice of accepting what 'is'. Acceptance brings peace into our lives.

There is a trap here and like many traps it arises from a lack of scrutiny. It's the trap of blind obedience, the trap of acquiescing one's freedom to an idea or ideal.

For the followers of many spiritual ways, blind obedience or faith brings them to moments of bliss. The faithful relish these moments and learn nothing about what 'is', instead they learn to seek and follow more of these moments of bliss. They get attached to the bliss instead of opening to the truth.

However, when the road gets rocky and the bliss fades, the seeker finds that faith and bliss prove a poor guide for life's journey. In truth, bliss is just like the sunshine receding behind the clouds and just like the clouds the bliss is always there. Peace, like the sunshine is a matter of perspective not faith.

The faithful catch the essence of letting go but miss its deeper meaning. Faith is like the mystics, it is not the thing, it's what it points to that interests us. A true spiritual life is not based on any beliefs it is only ever based on a knowing of the truth. This knowing can only be first-person, if you have faith as your 'way' then you can never know what 'is', you can glimpse it perhaps, yet never 'be' it.

The 'Way Within' offers you a way around this trap, it transforms this acceptance of what 'is' from an act faith and product of will to an immutable truth that comes from direct experience. There's nothing to be had from blindly trusting someone else's word for it. Don't 'think' your way, don't 'trust' your way. No, no, 'see' it and know it for yourself!

This is what Buddha meant when he said don't take a word he said on trust but instead scrutinize it like a goldsmith would when given a piece of gold. Weighing it, judging its color and testing its softness. He didn't mean doubt things, he meant look for yourself, see what 'is', be wise and act in wisdom not ignorance.

THE TRAP OF PURPOSE

There's another trap that seekers can't help but fall into. The very act of seeking is a trap. Goals are a trap. Expectations are a trap. What you want is a trap. Desires are a trap.

Each time we set our mind to something we are snagged. We are seeking for 'me', not seeing from 'I'.

Every goal has its roots in the ego and to make matters worse every effort to get something only feeds the ego. Each step on desires path strengthens the ego and takes you away from liberation.

This is the ego's game. However, understanding the ego's game reveals the ego's end. The ego's very source of strength is also its Achilles' heel.

The end comes if we stop playing the ego's game, it's that simple. The end of ego comes by playing a different game. No more hide and seek. The game we play as part of the 'Way Within' is the game of the anthropologist. We can't beat the ego, but we can watch, we can be the observer. An anthropologist is an observer that is never interested in the outcome of the scene. The anthropologist is always detached from events, the anthropologist is always detached for the events she observes. Instead, she's simply curious about what happens. You must quietly observe, be a witness that dispassionately sits back and lets events unfold. No judgement, no good or bad, no interference, no interest in outcomes, no bias, no hopes; just quite listening.

Play this game enough, and the ego will get weaker, cracks will appear, and a time will come when the early cracks finally break it up. What follows is enlightened peace and quiet. You are left with what 'is'. From here you truly know that "All is well, and all shall be well, and all manner of things shall be well".

Then a new game can start, but more on that later!

BEING THE UNIVERSAL WILL

If we get what we want, what we really want, there will be no stress and we will be happy. The obstacle to this in our everyday life is the disparity between what we think we want, and what we really want. This is further aggravated because we tend to keep shifting what we think we want onto something else.

In other words, we are kept from peace while we live in-authentically and keep looking for happiness in something else.

Your journey requires that you embrace the three wills and to live from zero distance. This starts by observing what you think you want, what you really want and ends by realizing what the universe wants.

YOUR CHALLENGE

The challenge now for you is to experience life as it 'is'. The challenge is never about grasping spiritual concepts. It's for you to know the peace of loving what 'is' and knowing this peace as what you really want. Furthermore, it's for you to know that what 'is' is what you intended! The challenge is knowing that 'what-is' is your will, and your 'will', will be done.

From your center, you'll come to know that intending 'what-is' is your immutable truth and it is this which reconciles the three wills and ultimately places your peace beyond any threat of fear. Ultimate peace comes when you go beyond merely acknowledging the universal will and start being the universal will.

THE 'WAY-SHOWERS' GIFT

For me, it's a beautiful thing to hold someone's hand as they slowly wake up to who they are. To be a way-shower and to do it in awareness is a wonderful thing! I would love to hold your hand as you wake up into awareness.

Most of all I would like to pass on this gift to you. When you come to awareness, you will become a 'way-shower'. Fact is, in awareness it's all but impossible to avoid becoming a 'way-shower' and this is big part of your journey now.

THE PROBLEM OF WORDS

Life is full of paradoxes. Awareness gifts you the reconciliation of life's paradoxes. Personally, as I awoke into awareness, I had a great urge to talk about my experience in all its sublime ordinariness, but of course there are no words.

You know what they say about mystics, "He who tells doesn't know, and he who knows doesn't tell." You've probably heard that or something similar quoted too many times. So, why in full knowledge of the paradox am I writing about awareness?

If the subject of this book is ineffable, how can I find words to illuminate it? Why am I encouraging you to take your turn and become a way-shower for others?

Well, the truth is that writing about this mystery, writing about the Tao, is just so delicious. It's the ultimate challenge for a writer. The challenge is that I can't tell you of the mystery, because there are no words, and in any case the second problem is that if you take my words and try to turn them into awareness; you'll turn them into stone.

If you try to make anything of my words they will weigh you down and you'll be drowned by them. You'll drown in my existence rather than swimming in your own awareness.

It's not just my words, it's all the words, all the ideas you've caught along the way. Much of your path is about dropping the attachments you've crafted from all the words you've studied, all the things you've been taught. It's about letting go of all the mill stones that have dragged you down, so you can float back to the surface and fill your lungs with air.

BE THE LESSON NOT THE TEACHER

As you awaken you'll be tempted to try to tell people what you know and show them how to apply this knowledge in their lives. As you begin the practice of awareness you'll want to solve their problems and remove the fear. You'll want this partly because you'll see it all so clearly and partly because you just want to help.

You'll want all this, you'll try, and you will fail.

However, if instead of preaching, teaching and meddling you just live as you are, just be. Then people will come to know through you the possibility, and in time they will come to you to know more. When they approach you, then you can point them to the truth so that they too can see what 'is' for themselves.

So, my suggestion is that you take a leaf out of this book and don't tell anyone anything. Instead, show them, help them to know it all for themselves. Be a way-shower, not a teller. Be the way, let people look where your life is pointing.

ALL IS WELL, ALL IS WHOLE

It's funny, although my words can't tell you directly, the paradox is that everything, absolutely everything in the universe, reveals the truth, even my words. The big joke is that everything is shouting out what can't be said. If you can look past the words and noise then you'll see what 'is', you'll see 'this', 'that' and 'everything'.

The wholeness of the universe is in everything and everything is whole. Awareness is everything, awareness is indivisible, awareness is in me, and therefore everything is in me and everything is in you too. The trick here, indeed the corner stone of our philosophy and the purpose of this book is to get you to look for yourself. It's not about any knowledge or understanding it's just about seeing, loving and being.

Your journey is to look inside and see all things springing from the 'no-thing' that is 'all things'. It's for you to be the un-knowable from which the known is born.

Try to see words in the same way that you are trying to observe your thoughts, let them come let them wash over you and let them go, don't cling to them don't make them into attachments. Don't try to be a master of words and ideas. Because this is no mastery, it's slavery. It's a death sentence that keeps you from the freshness of the eternal now.

I'm not making you come to awareness. I'm not going to tell you how to become enlightened or waste a moment of my time on such a totally indulgent and fruitless scheme. However, my ambition is that you will come to awareness and you'll come to know the peace of loving what 'is' and you'll do it by yourself and for yourself.

Your journey is to join me in loving what 'is'!

The profound truth is that, what 'is', is not merely OK, it's perfect. To quote Julian of Norwich again, "All is well, and all shall be well, and all manner of things shall be well".

It's great to be what we are, what happens now is perfect. Paradoxically, it's OK to try to be what we are not, to 'fake it'. If faking it is what we do, then it of itself has 'is-ness' and is the truth of your present moment. It's OK too, to try to change what 'is' to what 'is not'.

However, it's unlikely that any of these approaches will make you happy or bring peace into your life. All this is your journey for now, it's probably the wrong path to take, but that's not for me to say, that's something for you to discover.

There's often many wrong turns before we finally find our way home, it's just part of the process. Most of us only seem to learn the hard way, fortunately life patiently presents the same lesson over and over until we finally get it and move on. Such is life. Life can seem cruel, but life is not cruel, life is love, the love a father has for a child. The love of total intimacy.

Don't be hard on yourself, don't have regrets! Instead of regret and recrimination learn what life is revealing, celebrate each lesson, be grateful and wake from your slumbers.

DON'T THINK YOU'RE A FOOL, KNOW IT

My message, is don't fall for the trap of recrimination. This often follows on from when you realize that you're being less than ideal. Sometimes you'll think that you're just not measuring up to the standards you'd expect of yourself. Sometimes you're just doing something stupid. The recrimination comes when you realize your 'mistake' and get annoyed at yourself for being less than you hoped. You beat yourself up for it.

The not measuring up is a fault in your thinking not reality. You're just being human, being unaware, and that's fine, it's normal. If you do notice you're less than ideal, if you realize that you're acting without awareness, that's great. It should be a source of celebration, because subsequently into the void comes awareness.

I love it when that happens. I was a fool before awareness, then I'm in awareness and I 'know' I'm a fool. The difference is now I'm a fool with a smile on my face and a twinkle back in my eye.

It's madness to dive into recriminations. These thoughts take you further from awareness. When you beat yourself up you're a fool, only this time you 'think' you're a fool. This time instead of a smile you frown and you scowl at the world.

Sometimes seekers fall foul of what's called the *second error*. The first error is when we beat ourselves up for not being aware. The second error, is occurs when we subsequently beat ourselves up for beating ourselves up. How insane to beat our self for making innocent mistakes? This is a movement from unawareness to unawareness.

It's tragic, because each innocent mistake is a potential gateway to awareness. Each mistake is a gateway to the experience of seeing yourself as you are, as a fool. If you're not careful, you can beat yourself up for beating yourself up about beating yourself up. That would be the *third error* and the recriminations, if uninterrupted, can go on into infinity.

The thing to realize is that your foolishness is not a problem. It's a gateway to awareness. It's a movement from unawareness to awareness! You're being given two doors, one leads to awareness and bliss, the other to illusion, egotism and bitterness.

Guess which door the ego is ushering you towards? A blue pill or a red pill, which one will you take? It's time to choose and remember doing nothing is a choice!

NOT AWARE, NOT NOW

Trying to be what you are not (faking it) or changing *what-is* (denial) makes no sense in awareness. If you are trying to be what *you are not* or if you're trying to alter reality, then you are not being aware in that moment. In other words, you're not present. You're not in the 'now'!

Therefore, observation is so important. As the watcher, you see through the games you get drawn into playing. You see through the games the ego plays. Seeing though your charades, leaving them alone is the key. Leaving them alone causes all your illusions to fade. You're left with what you are and what 'is'. This is bliss! This is living in the 'now'.

Your journey in life is to the 'holy instant', to the 'now'. You're going home and you're going now! This is a journey of no distance and no time. The irony is, that you are already there, you just didn't *know* it.

SEPERATION IS OK, NON-DUALITY IS PERFECT

The whole 'OK', 'not OK' thing suggests duality, but with awareness we see that there is no duality, no right or wrong, no good or bad, no up or down.

We are not separate we are whole, we are one and all is well.

This is *OK*, this is *not OK*. In awareness, there is just 'isness' and all 'is'. Nothing is *OK*, nothing is *not OK*. Everything just 'is'. The illusion is created by what we add to what 'is'. The illusion is our judgement of what 'is' as being either *OK* or *not OK*.

You're *OK*, you're *not* OK is non-sense, you just are. If I say that you're *OK,* then I'm judging you. I'm adding my judgement to reality. In awareness you're neither, *OK* or *not OK*, you just are.

The *OK, not OK* thing is a product of ego, it has nothing to do with the truth or reality. The truth, is always just 'is' it is never *OK* or *not OK*.

Your reality is a product of awareness. In awareness reality is what 'is.' Whereas, in unawareness reality is *OK*, or it is *not OK*. In un-awareness reality is right or wrong depending on your unique brain-washing. Reality is based on your beliefs and thoughts, it's not based on the un-besmirched 'isness' of what 'is'.

I'm with Anthony De Mello when he says, "I'm an Ass, you're an Ass and it's *OK*." For me, it's not just *OK* to be an ass, it's perfect! Incidentally, if you ever meet me remember this and we'll get on fine! No pedestals please, just humble God meeting God!

Your journey is to be perfect, which is what you are. You're perfect even if you're an Ass, and you are an Ass, so let's get over it. We will more than just get over it. We will join in oneness if you just stick with it. Stick with it and you'll discover that you are perfect, and you always have been.

Through awareness we come to experience oneness with all and know the perfection of all.

Once you see that you are not separate from the rest of creation, once you see for yourself that creation is perfect, you rarely ever see yourself as anything other than what you are, perfect and whole.

THE LESSONS OF KNOWLEDGE?

WHAT'S YOUR SPATIAL AWARENESS LIKE?

IF I ASKED you, "Where are you?" I'm guessing that most of you know where you are, right? I'm on a train going through Kings Langley at around 100mph. You might be sitting at home in Princeton.

Are you comfortable with that? But where is Princeton? Well, if you're in Princeton then you know that Princeton is in Mercer county, which is in New Jersey, which is in the United States of America, which is on planet Earth, which is orbiting the sun as part of the solar system, which in turn is somewhere in the Milky Way. If you're a keen astronomer you might be able to go further, but sooner or later you're going to run out of points of reference.

So, if you take a moment to think about this, you'll have to admit that you're left with a limited and at best an abstract sense of where you are.

I'm suggesting that you really don't know where you are. At least in an absolute sense you don't.

If you're not with me on this think about the universe. We are told it's infinite and ultimately unknowable in its entirety and at the universe's extremes (relative to where you are) it is moving away from us faster than the speed of light.

In the end, you must admit that where you are in this vastness is totally unknowable. It's as if you can know what's on your doorstep, but not where the doorstep is.

TIME TRAVEL

We tend to look at the universe and our own lives through the lens of time. For our physical selves, time is a one-way arrow, our bodies move along times arrow and in this respect, we are totally trapped in time. We experience a life moment by moment, always physically now, always physically present until we reach our end and experience oblivion.

Unlike our bodies, our thoughts are not tied to time's arrow or the present moment. In fact, for many of us our thoughts are never in the now.

Our attention can be directed at will. However, is often directed to either past events or worries of a possible future. Our train of thought often moves seemingly with a will of its own to dwell on the past or ponder the future, but rarely does it rest for long in the present moment.

The quality of our life is directly related to how good we are at directing our attention.

If you spend most of your time dwelling on the past or fearing the future the quality of your life is going to be poor. However, if you direct your attention to where it needs to be, which is almost exclusively in the present moment, then the quality of your life will be high.

There's nothing wrong with looking back or projecting forwards, the problem is when your attention is totally out of your control and not fulfilling a current need.

Thinking is healthy when it is aligned to a need you have now. Thinking is unhealthy when it is running amok thinking random stuff or commenting on events that may or may not have happened.

You could say the problems of thought arise when your attention is not aligned with your physical body; which is always present, always now.

If on the other hand your attention is firmly in the present moment and when called for thought is directed at will to the past to help with the present challenge or to look forward and so plan your preferred outcomes. Then you will experience a totally different quality of life. You will be aligned both physically and mentally.

In the present, there is nothing wrong, no fear, nothing that you cannot deal with. In the past there are doubts, regrets and general deceptions. In the future lays the fear of the possible, uncertainty, failure and death.

WHAT'S THE QUALITY OF YOUR LIFE?

Do you drift between memories, worrying about what you did, what you didn't do? Do you worry about what's coming down the line, what people might do or what people might not do?

Or are you present in almost every moment, delighted by the mystery as things unfold, always ready to do what's needed and always at peace?

I don't know about you, but I've spent most of my life out of control, though I've had times of total presence and I certainly know which I prefer and which I'm choosing now.

WHAT IS THE TIME?

We take for granted that time is something we can know. Ask yourself: What time is it? What is the time? Easy, for me it's 06:29 GMT, right? When is that? June 19th, 2013! So, when is that? Already, I'm a bit lost, then I remember that it's about 2013 years after a bunch of people ascribe to the birth of Jesus.

I'm feeling a pretty loose grip on exactly when it is. If I pull back and look at all time and ponder time from a universal scale, where is now in all of time. I'm completely lost. Is now near the beginning, in the middle or at the end of all time? Does anything make any sense if time is infinite?

Physicists or mathematicians might say this is a meaningless line of reason and that we are thinking of the infinite in finite terms, which is true but whatever the logic or reason my sense of disorientation is acute.

PAYING ATTENTION TO TIME AND MIND

I spoke earlier about how our attention is not tied to time in the same way that our physical bodies seem to be, and to illustrate this right now, this moment I can place my awareness in the past or future. In much the same way, I can also put my attention in the mind of another, I can think from another person's point of view.

In my experience, there are three main causes of misery in the world. These are: dwelling on the past, worrying about the future and dwelling on what other people may or may not be thinking.

Just like placing my attention in the future or dwelling on the past, thinking what someone else is thinking about, is swapping reality in all its perfection, for an illusion.

While it can be interesting and useful to try to have empathy for another person's situation. What other people may be thinking or for that matter what other people might be doing is none of our business.

THREE TYPES OF STUFF

One of the most insightful people on this topic is Byron Katie. She makes life so simple by pointing out that there are only three types of stuff in the world:

1. My stuff
2. Your stuff
3. God's stuff

She also tells us that two out of the three are none of our business! It's obvious when I say it, but your stuff and God's stuff is none of my business and every moment I spend thinking about your stuff or God's stuff, I'm dealing in things that are none of my business. When I get caught up in other stuff I'm distracted from my life, I've traded reality for an illusion, I've swapped peace and happiness for fear and loathing.

When you think about it for a minute you'll find that most of your troubles, and the troubles you have witnessed, were due to thinking about other people's stuff or worrying about God's stuff; about which we can know nothing.

Our troubles get compounded when we add things to reality. Trouble starts when we add thoughts, attributes, qualities, meaning, values and a general sense that it should be other than it is.

I'm not saying don't drift into other people's stuff or God's stuff. However, in the tradition of Byron Katie I would suggest that you gently ask yourself what would your life be like if you didn't dwell on other people's stuff or worry about God's stuff?

WHAT CAN YOU KNOW?

WHAT DO I KNOW?

TO BE FRANK, I know nothing! The irony is that this might be the only thing I can ever know. This insight comes from one of the few things that I understand, which is about what I don't know.

I don't know where I am, and I don't know when it is. When I look down at the world I can't find a thing that I can absolutely say I know. When I consider the objects around me I realize that I can't find anything of substance; lots of appearance but nothing solid!

It's funny, coming from someone like me, that's spent almost half a century learning stuff. You see my experience is that these days, when I ask a couple of questions, I quickly come to the point of the unknown. I come to nothing.

To see what I mean, consider this. If I look at the table and see its wood, it appears solid, it's a table. However, if I were to look closer I'd see wood molecules. Looking closer still I'd see the atoms that make up the wood molecules. Moving closer, I'd see the particles that are the atoms basic building blocks and when I examine these atoms I'd see mostly space. The atoms I'd see are far from solid and seen from this distance are more like mini solar systems with a few planet like particles orbiting in a vast empty space around a tiny central nucleus.

So, this table is not solid at all, it's almost entirely empty space. It has the appearance of being solid at the material level and mostly empty space at the sub atomic level.

Then what of the particles that give the impression of solidness and reality. Of these I can know nothing, as soon as I look at them the very act of looking changes them.

Don't panic if you're feeling like you're looking directly into the abyss. It's not all bad. In fact, it's not bad at all as everything flows from nothing. The unknowable is manifest and the 'Way Within' brings mastery of the void.

The best that science offers us is a probabilistic model of reality, one that isn't solid, and it certainly isn't absolute knowledge. The best science can say is that on balance a particle will probably do 'this', but if you watch the same particle it will respond to being watched by doing 'that'.

We like to think that the things we have are made of something but on examination they are made of nothing. Nothing is the source of everything.

At its heart the universe is a web of uncertainty where for any particle you can either know it's direction, velocity or position, but never all three at the same time. In other words, we can never know exactly where any particle is, where it's come from, where it's going to and at what speed it's moving.

If we take this insight as the foundation on which all understanding of the physical must be built i.e. where it is, where it's going and at what speed it is going there. Then everything that we think we know is tenuous and can't be deemed absolute knowledge. Nothing in the real world, can ever be more than a theory, concept or handy approximation of how things are.

Nothing is real.

It really is as if God plays dice, only he throws them where we can't see them and annoyingly he won't tell us what numbers come up.

Nothing is known.

In my experience, I can find no matter, neither in the world nor in my awareness. It seems that increasingly when scientists look, they too can find no matter, they just find modulations emerging from nothing and slipping back into nothing like bubbles in a clear glass of soda.

WHAT DO YOU KNOW?

So, what is it that you really know? Humor me here for a bit and look. All you have do is to ask the simplest questions like how, where, etc.? Ask yourself:

- How has that happened?
- How do you know that's true?
- Where did that come from?
- Why did that happen?

Keep repeating the questions. Keep peeling the onion until you come to the point of your not knowing.

Even if you are studious and want to do some research you'll quickly come to the point that science doesn't know. Then beyond whatever knowledge you can glean, the theories sooner or later breakdown and you come to the unknowable. You find yourself in the place where God plays dice.

Similarly, if you look out into the ever-expanding universe you will reach a point beyond which knowledge is not possible. You reach a point where the universe beyond is moving away from you faster than the speed of light. The consequence of this is that no light, no information of distant events, can ever reach us from these distant parts of the universe. These far places disappear behind an information horizon. For us they fall into darkness. For anyone beyond the event horizon reality continues in all its wonderful colors and light and we, in our distant galaxy, fall into darkness.

In the place of anything solid, at best you have lots of theories of what reality is, and how stuff works. You have theories that are all stacked on top of each other with nothing solid to under pin them.

It's easy to mistake our beliefs for reality. It's easy to assume our thinking is based on something solid when all we have is the belief in something solid. Beliefs that are underpinned by layers of theories, most of them unknown to the believer and all of them flawed.

Don't panic, it's not a problem as the theories work well enough in practice. You turn on your TV and it works. You don't need to understand the theory of Quantum Electro Dynamics to watch the Game of Thrones.

Theories make it possible to do the most amazing things. However, even more amazing things are possible when you see through the veil of theory to the deeper truth beyond.

WHERE ARE YOU NOW?

If you agree with me, you'll have to conclude that part and parcel of your great ignorance is a complete lack of knowledge of where you are.

Fact is, you can't say in an absolute sense where here is. However, you can have awareness of where your attention is moment by moment.

Again, don't panic. You don't need deep knowledge of the whole universe. You don't need absolute or even relativistic knowledge of your position in terms of time or space. Knowing where you are in an everyday sense and what the time of day, week, month and year is plenty good enough to get by.

Knowing where all things are, is God's business not yours, relax and leave him to do it all. Instead, bring your attention to this moment and do what needs to be done with awareness.

When you're doing the dishes, be there for them and you'll find love and bliss. If the dishes are before you and your hands are scrubbing away keep your attention right here don't ponder the universe, or worry about what someone did or didn't do or is going to do. Be here, be now miracles await you! Dishes will be done. However, you won't find anyone doing them, when you really look you observe there's only peace and happiness. Here and now there are no more tasks, no more chores but all things are done.

DIRECT EXPERIENCE

It seems that there is nothing that we can know, other than where our attention is. However, there is much that we can experience. We can experience the direction of our attention, are we thinking about the future, reflecting on the past, enjoying the moment, imagining another's thought process.

What in our field of experience are we focused on, I was looking at my cup of tea, then listening to the train guard announcing our arrival at Watford.

I can never know a cup of tea, but I can experience it. I can be aware of it. The cup can be a small peripheral part of my awareness or with focus it can fill up awareness. Ask yourself these questions: What can I know? What do I know?

When you think of something that you know, ask yourself, "Is this really true in an absolute sense"?

I think it's quite paradoxical that the key to answering the question is awareness and the answer is awareness too. The answer you are looking for is awareness. Awareness, awareness, awareness!

Coming back to the cup of tea with these questions I realize that I don't know the cup at all. What I know is my experience of the cup. The image of the cup appears in awareness. For me the cup is never known in a direct sense. I never see the cup, I have the experience of seeing the cup in awareness. I never touch the cup, I have the experience in awareness of touching the cup. It is just known in awareness. In this moment, I'm aware of my knowing of the cup. Likewise, all my thoughts about the cup also appear in the same field of awareness.

PARADOX OF EXPERIENCE

It seems like life is a paradox, where everything we think of as real, everything we think of as objective, as substantial, turns out to be totally unknowable. The irony is that the subjective, in other words, what's experienced internally, is all that we can call real. The cup has no reality beyond the knowing of the cup.

The ultimate paradox is that as soon as we try to know things, by which I mean to attach any knowledge to our experiences, they are thrown into question. In contrast, the experience 'as-it-is', pure, without anything added, is the only reality available to you. The only truth!

I'm looking at an everyday scene. I'm seeing a man running to get a train, but it's an illusion. To get a sense of what I mean, a few moments after seeing the man running for the train, the illusion is revealed when we realize that he's running to catch a child that's strayed. We saw a man and we attached meaning to what we saw, we assumed as he was at railway station and because he was running he must be running for a train.

Don't get caught up with all this nonsense. Don't be beguiled by what I'm saying. It's all just words. Later, if you hang around I'll help you to the place where all experience unfolds so that you can know that place and all experiences for yourself.

Don't worry about trying to understand or arrange these ideas and concepts into some sort of intellectual framework. The old approach to learning things that worked so well in school and at work won't help you now!! It will just create more baggage that you'll only have to work to get rid of later!

When you see, all will be revealed in its simplicity and perfection.

VICTIM OR CREATOR, YOUR CHOICE!

Nothing has meaning of itself, nothing means anything, and there is only the meaning you give to things. For us, there is no absolute knowledge, nothing can be known about anything other than it 'is'.

Where does that leave you? Are you feeling a bit lost in a world without absolutes, a world without meaning to cling on to?

Clearly things are not as we'd assumed. So, if there is no meaning, save what you give things, it becomes clear that you have a very big role in reality. It implies that you are the creator of the world you experience.

If this is true, and it is, this means that what you create is either heaven or hell with no in-betweens. The doors to the kingdom of heaven are here, and now, and they are open. It's a kingdom of choices and freedom, where you get to choose everything. This truly is heaven on earth. This is liberation!

In this way, it's perhaps more accurate to say that you create illusion, not reality and illusion becomes your reality. You create heaven by leaving reality as it is. There's more to this, as we will see later because you not only create illusions you co-create reality.

We keep looking for more when with seeing we have what 'is' what more could you need? Nothing!

NOT THINKING, BEING

Don't get too hung up on this, just now. It's enough to know that you have awareness, and awareness is to know that the thoughts you have are not real. The thoughts you have just color the picture and you don't have to get caught by every thought. You don't have to get taken in by your thoughts, you don't have to be 'thought', you can be aware and watch your thoughts from a distance.

If you get caught by a thought, that's fine because now you know not to take thoughts too seriously, and sooner or later you will remember that it's just a thought. Your thought has no meaning, it doesn't change what is happening unless you let it. You can have another thought and create another reality.

The insight here is that this way of being is the source of all freedom. If you can live with life as it 'is', you will find peace, happiness and your purpose in life.

WHERE DOES THIS LEAVE ME?

THE WAY WITHIN - THE WAY FORWARDS

IT LEAVES YOU with a way forward! It's not a matter of learning anything. Trust me, you know everything you need to know. No, it leads you to direct experience or perhaps more accurately it leaves you with direct experience.

You can read more books, I can sit down and tell you things about how it is for me, some teacher or guru can tell you what to do, but this is all just information being transferred. What's worse as the information settles in your mind it turns into theories or concepts that are poor imitations of the truth.

The 'Way Within' isn't about learning anything or mastering stuff. The 'Way Within' got you to embrace life, it helped you via direct experience to gain understanding, appreciation and love. In short, you must follow the pointers and see for yourself. You must bring this life into direct experience. Most of us live life at a distance, by proxy in a dream. It doesn't have to be like that, you can wake up.

Learning and reading are wonderful, but they are poor substitutes for wisdom. Wisdom is manifest not in what you know but in what you do, and it can only happen in the now.

We need a new way of approaching life. If we can't rely on what we think, we must look at what we really do know. When we eliminate everything that is unknowable we are left with only one thing of any solidity and real value. Direct experience, your personal first-person experience. It turns out that we can only know the world as it unfolds in awareness.

Incidentally, I call my philosophy, efformism; because my approach gets to reality by accepting what we can't know (the ineffable) and directing our attention to what we can know (the effable) and doing so through direct first-person experience. Efformism underpins the 'Way Within'.

We can't know our true nature through logic, reason, it can't be written or taught, but we can look for ourselves and know it through first-person experience.

The only knowable is the experience of awareness.

YOU'RE MISSING SOMETHING!

Later in the book we are going to look together at what we see with attention and awareness. When we look, it's interesting what you can't see. It's so obvious, it had been staring me in the face but until I was prompted by Richard Lang I'd never have known what was missing from my view.

I'd probably never had noticed if I'd not been at a headless workshop with Richard guiding my attention. With his help, when I looked at what 'is' I too was struck by what's missing. When I looked, I realized I've no head just a big space where my head should be. The trick, is to look at what you see as you look at the world and only accept what is there. Now I know I've got a big head with an inane grinning face that greets the world, but when I look I should go with what I see and there's no head. I see a head there across the table, as someone I've never seen before looks out of the train window at rural Hertfordshire.

It seems, I've spent my whole life imagining things here, but what's here, right here is just capacity for whatever I'm presented with. What we will be learning to do is seeing exactly what is here for me, and there for you. Got it?

Don't worry, this is not about ideas and concepts, it' just about looking and seeing, in the end you'll realize that nothing could be easier!

This is another big lesson. The truth is not what you expect to see, or what you are imagining, it's just what you experience!

This isn't new news, it's what the mystics have been telling us for thousands of years. This 'seeing' is the practice that's at the heart of all mysticism. Please don't worry, there's nothing hard to get your head around. There's a simple set of exercises that we will follow, and these exercises will enable you to see what the mystics saw. This is great news as it brings the essence of mystical experience to the masses, whereas the mystics were at the mercy of God and many had to make super human sacrifices to achieve their revelations. The irony is of course that the universe doesn't ask anything from you, no sacrifices are required, but if you are present and open to it then miracles flow, you flow.

THE GENIE'S OUT OF THE BOTTLE

I've been so used to a face here where now I find just space. Now I realize that there was never a face here, it was a stopper that kept my infinite capacity bottled up. Now I've seen the truth of who I am, I'm not that face I see over there, in the mirror. No, I'm spacious capacity for all. I have no limits, no end and only peace and love rule this space. Once the genie is out of the bottle, there's no limit on your potential and miracles rapidly become the new order of the day.

HOW FAR ARE YOU FROM WHAT YOU EXPERIENCE?

When you stop putting stuff between yourself and your experience, when you look in to your very center and explore what fills your being, you will find no distance between you and the experiences you have. You find oneness is what you are, there is no separation, no subject-object duality.

I don't know about you, but most people are not at center. Most people are a bit removed from center, quite a bit removed. Most people, and I would say all unenlightened people, are the face they present to the world.

When you look out from the face that you present to the world, though you seem to be looking from a few inches from center you have in effect placed a world of knowledge between you and the experience of life.

In contrast, when you look from your center you start to see that you are everything and everything is you. From a few inches, you have set yourself apart and you will be forever separate. From zero distance, there is no boundary between you and what you experience. At your center, you will find the oneness you've been seeking.

THE WORLD YOU CREATE

I'm guessing you're familiar with the idea of projection. You're probably familiar with the idea that the world that you see, and experience reflects your own beliefs, thoughts and feelings. However, this projection is not truth. You have added something, something that's not there. This something you are adding is the fiction of 'you', it's what you know as 'me.'

Everything that's wrong in the world is just a reflection of what you believe is wrong with you. Know this, there is nothing wrong with you. You are perfect, you always were. Sadly, you just didn't know it. I love you!

BEWARE OF MANIFESTING YOUR EGO

There's much written about manifestation and about how what you believe, think and feel can manifest reality. The *Law of Attraction* has become an obsession for many. The problem is that if you try to use the *Law of Attraction* you will not be manifesting from a place of truth, love and oneness.

The *Law of Attraction* is a two-sided sword. The *Law of Attraction* has potential to move us along our path or it can send us down a deep dark dead end. The point is we should be careful what we wish for. We should also observe and note what we wish for.

Until you have left your seeking behind you will always be manifesting your ego. Until then, the things you long for are the things that will support the fiction of you, the fiction that you're trying to project onto the world.

When you live from center, in the now, you will manifest what you are without trying. You will bring forth only love, peace and truth.

GO EASY ON YOUR EGO

In society, it's normal to look for someone to blame. When we come to looking at how our life is the ego can appear to be a bit of a problem. It's not surprising then that for a lot of people the ego is the bad guy and they feel they are the victim of its evil machinations.

The truth is that the ego is innocent of all crimes. When you look at what happens you'll see that the ego doesn't exist before a feeling. Ego is just the movement of thoughts that we attach 'me' to.

The ego 'thought' only appears after an event occurs. It is never present in the now. When seen like this it's clear that there is no ego as such and if the ego doesn't exist before the experience, how can it be responsible for anything.

If there is no ego, then we're just left with the movement of thoughts. If you look where I'm pointing, you'll start to see how you're like a mirror. For you, thoughts will increasingly be nothing more than fleeting images, and just like a mirror, once the source of the reflection has gone you will be perfectly unchanged. Just like a mirror, once your thoughts have passed, you'll be left totally unaffected by them.

Before awareness we're like a movie where our thoughts are made into scenes and we keep playing the gory ones over and over. Stick with me and drop the drama and in its place, you will find peace and happiness.

SEEKERS AND SEEKING MANIFESTATION

For seekers, the *Law of Attraction* is rarely a fruitful way. We should be careful what we wish for, don't wish for things, power or change. You might well get them. However, you won't get what you are really looking for. Instead, you will move further from where you need to be.

Getting things, seeking power or making changes never transform you, they can never make you happy. At best the things you get just give you a buzz, a thrill or they temporarily shake life up a bit. None of that lasts long.

When you leave seeking behind and you find that you can see, then you're a seer. Once you see you can live in aware freedom. With your very next thought, you can become a sage. Liberation can be yours, if you just wish for things to be exactly as they are. It's yours if you accept all things exactly as they are. The ultimate intimacy is love. Love what 'is' and be free.

When you see, you will begin to realize that you, as spacious capacity, are always accepting everything. But giving yourself over to this revelation may take time. This surrender is the essence of what it is to be a sage, and as a sage you will wish for life to flow through you. This is the next step on the 'Way Within' from seer to sage.

For now, wish to be stronger, not for things to be easier. Wish to learn to love things as they are. Pray for a miracle. The miracle I recommend you ask for, is that you give yourself up to the will of God. Stop praying for things to be different, stop asking for things to be given you, stop hoping for God's will to be bent to serve your whims and wishes. That's crazy.

Stop trying to manifest what 'is not' and instead love what 'is'.

THE FLOW OF LIFE

People see the *Law of Attraction* as a tool to direct the flow of life. The big mistake is to think that you know what is best. The mistake we make is to try to hang onto the good times and will more good times and things into being.

The beautiful truth is that good times like all things come and go. If we hang onto them for even a moment of direct the flow of life we corrupt it.

A better approach is to gaze into the void and greet what the universe brings forth with love, awe and gratitude. Marvel at the miraculous way the universe provides what we really need; which is rarely what we imagined we needed.

THE UPSIDE OF PROJECTION

If you give projection some attention you'll realize that when you observe what you have been experiencing, you are observing what's inside not what's outside.

What's revealed is what's between you and reality. Though this observation of yourself, you can start to perceive the lens through which you've been looking at the world.

For most of us this lens is forever behind the veil. Once you see for yourself you can let it go! You can literally take off the old cloudy glasses and see clearly.

To help you to see clearly, we'll use some simple techniques later in the book that will lay bare this inner landscape and allow you to turn it around.

The most wonderful things flow from you when you strip the world of your thoughts and beliefs. Things flow when you let them go.

BE AWARE OF WHAT YOU'RE ADDING, AND MIRACLES WILL HAPPEN

For now, try to be aware of what you're adding to the world. Awareness of what you're adding is a great start. You don't have to do anything more than watch things unfold. Watch where your thoughts are coming from, observe how they affect you. See how your thoughts add color and shade to the things you see and add feeling to the events that happen. Just watch without any desire to change anything. Watch without judging what you see. Watch like none of it affects you. Watch as though you are an unconcerned bystander.

Just watch, let it be, and before your eyes you will see miraculous creation unfold. The problems of old will start to be transformed without you doing anything other than observing while leaving the world unmolested!

ARE YOU TAKING THE LONGEST JOURNEY TO HERE?

Are you seeking? I ask because, if you're off seeking, then you're not here. But where are you?

In my experience, seekers don't find, because they are distracted by the journey. In a sense, they've inadvertently mistaken the road for the destination.

When I was deep into seeking, I was forever on the hunt for some new wisdom. Ironically, time and time again into my hands came great wisdom. Each time I saw it, and understood it, and I was excited by it, whether it was Katie Byron asking if I really knew it was true or Anthony DeMello getting me to see what an Ass I was. For all my understanding and despite the deep resonance with the insights that came to me, there was no wisdom. I wasn't wise because rather than doing a thing, rather than living the insight and sticking with it I was too busy buying and then greedily devouring the next book by the next person.

It's not just me, I know many of my friends suffer similarly. They hop from book to book, guru to guru and like dharma bums they traipse from one retreat to the next. Are you a dharma bum caught in the blinding light of seeking?

The destination you are seeking is not at the end of a path. Your destination is no distance at all, your destination is right here, right now! You see, you really don't need to pick up another book, or go to another workshop. You just need to open your eyes and see for a few minutes, right here, right now.

I'm offering you the pathless path, the 'No-Way' way. The logic is clear. There is no way that you can wander down that will take you to 'now'. There's no distance to cover, it's here. You are never anywhere else, other than here and it is never any other time than now. It's just your mind that wanders off.

I'm offering you a few pointers that will help you to wake up and get back to where you came from. Where all things come from and know that place. I'm offering you my hand, so take it and I'll come with you.

> *"We shall not cease from exploration, and the*
> *end of all our exploring will be to arrive where*
> *we started and know the place for the first time."*
>
> T. S. Eliot

ARE YOU PRESENT, ARE YOU GIVING?

If you're seeking you're not here. It's not a problem because we can let go of the past, leave the future alone and when you drop the past and leave the future you will be present. Where else can you be? Nothing could be simpler.

If you let go, you will come to understand that now is the only time there is. Leave the future, leave the past, and you'll discover this instant is for giving.

Are you home right now? Are you giving your all to every moment?

OTHER SIDESHOWS ON THE JOURNEY

It's not just dwelling in the past and pondering your future that keeps you away from home, there are many, many other side shows going on to distract you along the way. There are many traps that you can fall into and many of these traps are very comfortable. So, comfortable in fact, that you really won't want to get out of them.

Many spiritual practices can in themselves become attachments that though they may start you going in the right direction become a distraction from what they point to. They become substituted in your mind for what's pointed at. Be warned, any spiritual practice can catch you like this. Meditation is a great example of a practice that can easily become a trap. Don't confuse the finger with where it's pointing.

Spiritual experiences themselves are another trap for the unwary. Many people get addicted to the high, to the elation that sometimes accompanies a spiritual experience. They can become addicts. Don't confuse the bliss for what it is associated with. Bliss is never an attribute of the truth, it's just a feeling. Don't keep going back for more bliss, let the feelings go. Look where the bliss comes from, see what it points to, don't get stuck in it or blinded by it.

It's not just spiritual experiences that can trap you. For many people religion can be as much an obstacle as it is a way. Don't mistake the way for home. It's just the way, it's not the one. No religious book, no ritual or holy object is worth more than a human life. Nothing is more holy or precious than a life.

Sacrament is not the one. There are many paths, and all paths lead to the one but at the end you must leave the path, you must leave your religion and step into the one! No religious sacrament, relic or item is any more sacred than a leaf that falls from a tree, and none of them point any more clearly at the one than a humble falling leaf.

It's not just religion you you'll have to leave. You will have to leave all your beliefs. You'll have to leave everything to come home to the one!

Don't panic, you don't have to deny anything. You certainly don't have to expunge all traces of your beliefs. You don't have to give all your possessions to the poor or charity. You just need to let them go and in doing so you'll free yourself from your attachments.

It's your attachments that keep you from what you seek. Drop them one by one as you see them. Drop them when they come up and stand in your way.

ARE YOU RIGHT OR ARE YOU HAPPY?

How do you feel when you're right? Great, right? I know I used to!

By contrast think for a moment what it feels like when you are doing something you love. For me it's writing, for my friend Scott the moment comes when he's water-skiing. Whatever, it is that you love you have probably had that sense of being in the zone where nothing else exists because your absorbed just by the act of doing. You cease to be separate from what is happening.

Think about how it feels when something happens, and you just find yourself doing a good deed. No intention, nothing to gain, you just do a good deed. I'm sure you've had it happen many times. I'm sure you can recall how that feels.

Think about how it feels when you're in nature, maybe just looking at a beautiful seascape or absorbed by the way some mountains kiss the sky. Maybe you're watching the flight of a great bird. I'm sure you've been there and had this feeling of awe and peace.

Think about how it feels when you watch a beautiful sunset. I love the way the sun sets in Australia. For me, nothing I've ever seen can compare with the colors, the brilliance and the wonderful feelings that a Sunset in South Australia serves up, totally awesome.

Now, take a few minutes to think about the times you're right. Maybe, a friend and you have disagreed about something and eventually you've proved beyond doubt that you were correct, and he was wrong. You've proved that you were right and that he was wrong. He was wrong, wrong, wrong!

Dwell for a few moments on how it feels to be right when this happens.

Think about the times when you've been competing maybe in a game or sport and you finally win. How does it feel to win? How does it feel when you crush someone with your skills or your good luck tips the scales in your favor so that you come out on top? How does it feel when you hit the net cord at match point and the ball drops unhittable into your opponent's court? How does it feel when against the run of play your team steals a winning goal in the last minute of added time in a cup final?

Do you know the feelings I'm talking about?

It's not really awesome, and it's not really happy, it's sort of smug feeling and as I think about it it's hard to think that it's exactly good. It's the result of what they call a zero-sum game, you win I lose. You have dived into your separation, which always leaves you wanting more. It is a feeling defined by your innate sense of lack not your wholeness.

In contrast, how does it feel to be at one with nature, to watch the sunset, to be consumed with just doing what you love to do? You've not taken anything, you've joined something, and you felt the universe's infinite abundance. Nothing must be taken from anyone else, all must be given. You've experienced a taste of oneness. You've tasted the infinite and in that all your appetites are sated. No more longing! No more hunger for something else.

Well, more likely that you are full for a bit! Don't be surprised when hunger returns but the blessing is that now you know how to eat healthily in a way that will satisfy and nourish you and spread love.

In English, we have the expression "It's like chalk and cheese." For me this choice between being right or being happy is like "chalk and cheese." What do you want on your plate, chalk or cheese?

DO YOU WANT TO BE RIGHT OR HAPPY?

Ariel and Shya Kane in their book "Working on yourself doesn't work." talk about happiness as being a choice between two houses. In one house you can be right, in the other house you can be happy. You must choose which house you want to live in because you can't be right and be happy. You can't live in two houses at the same time.

If you take things to a deeper level, being right or wrong is an illusion. You can never be right, there's no right there's just 'is'. Each time you're right you're adding something to what 'is', your adding something that's of yourself and not of the thing you are experiencing.

The question is, "Are you in the happy house or the right house?" Where do you want to be, right or happy? For some of us this simple insight can be one of the great revelations in our life. Do I want to be happy, or do I want to be right? The choice you make will determine the quality and nature of your life. This can be a turning point in your life if you take the happy path, it will be a happy ending.

Ironically, it turns out authentic living lies not in doing what is right but in being happy. That's a hard pill for many of us to swallow as it seems to go against the moral imperative to do the right thing.

KNOWING NOTHING, KNOWING ME, KNOWING YOU

It's humbling to know nothing. However, it's not just humbling to know nothing. In the end knowing nothing is liberating. It is total liberation, total freedom.

I don't know where I am, when it is, where anything is or what anything is. I don't know what's right. I don't know what's right for me, what's right for you, what's right for anyone. I certainly don't know what's right for the world at large.

Phew, what a weight has fallen from my shoulders. No right house for me! I need to follow the bliss, everything that's left when you take away being right is bliss!

Paradoxically, when it all falls away, I do know, I know what 'is' and it is all right.

> *"All shall be well, and all shall be well, and all manner of things shall be well."*
>
> *Julian of Norwich*

When I think, I know something, I'm in fact deluding myself. I'm just seeing me in the way of the truth. At this level of awareness, I only experience 'me', and you only experience 'you'. Paradoxically, the more we experience ourselves, the more unaware of ourselves we are!

I can drop 'me', I can see past me and when I do I find the truth in full view. The 'me' is still there, it's just not a concern anymore. This 'me' thing is no more to me than a black hole at the center of a distant star system.

You too can drop your 'me,' you can see past yourself to the truth too. The truth's not hidden, its right here and right now.

The key to unlocking the paradox of 'me' is found in playing or rather not playing what Douglas Harding called the face game. You break free from playing the face game when you come to see that my face is not here for me, it's there for you. Your face is not there for you it's here for me! Come closer, fill my world with your face here for me and all I can see is me, but my face isn't here it's there!

Don't worry if this sounds a bit cryptic, all will be revealed later when you will get to explore this for yourself.

WHAT ARE YOU THINKING?

One thing about thoughts is that you can't change them! Don't think you can change a single thought!

Another thing about thoughts is that they can't change you either! They can affect how you feel and they can influence what you do, but they can't change you, nothing can change you.

These thoughts can change the story you tell about yourself. However, this story is just another thought, this thought is not you. Though it is what you have gotten used to thinking of as 'me'. You have become identified with a story of your own creation, a story that changes like the wind. You've identified with this fictional 'me' while totally ignoring the immutable 'I' that is your truth.

Take a moment to reflect on your thoughts and the impact they have. Are you being lived by your thoughts? Are your thoughts in charge? Do you believe what you think? Are you thinking or are you being thought?

I for one did believe my own thoughts, and what a mess it got me into. You wouldn't believe the mess thoughts got me into. Though, I'm sure that if you take a minute to think about your own life and the mess that your thoughts have created, you can perhaps start to imagine my mess.

DON'T BELIEVE A SINGLE THOUGHT

There's no truth in thoughts, don't believe a thing you think, watch your thoughts yes, use your thoughts, enjoy your thoughts and why not? However, don't surrender your life to them, they are not you!

Make no mistake, you can't change your thoughts and please don't try to as it will end badly. However, you can let them go, you can leave them be.

Have you tried to let your thoughts go or have you tried to stop them? Are you trying to change them? Are you trying to think them? Don't resist your thoughts, resistance makes them stronger. Accept them, watch them if you will and they will in their own time leave you in peace.

It's totally normal to try to stop 'bad' thoughts or change 'negative' thoughts, but the truth is neither of these things are possible. The way out of bad and negative thoughts is to either just leave them be, although most people never try this option. The other option is to swap one thought for another. Swapping thoughts is increasingly popular and is at the heart of things like: Neuro-Linguistic Programming (NLP), Speaking Therapies and Hypnotherapy. However, though replacing thoughts can be effective it comes with risks and is not consistent with the peaceful mind that we are looking for.

In contrast, letting your thoughts go, frees your mind for the next thought, it's liberating as opposed to swapping one prison cell for another more comfortable one.

The truth is that following hot on the heels of the insight that you know nothing, comes the realization that you can never know what the right thoughts are. Following this logic, how can you ever select the best thoughts to replace the old bad thoughts?

By closing your thoughts down, you are denying the magical creativity that will flow from an open mind. All things come from nothing and in good time all things return to nothing. By bringing silence to your mind you create the space for the creative force of the universe to materialize the insights, ideas and solutions you need. If you decide instead to fill your mind with new thoughts to push out what you judge to be bad thinking, you will stifle your mind not enhance it. You will block natures creative genius!

Silence is not the absence of sound. Silence is the absence of you.

WHAT AM I

What am I behind the thoughts?

When you watch your thoughts, when you watch the events of your life, when you watch your feelings who are you? Who is watching?

This watching self, this awareness behind the 'me,' this is where you will find the 'I' and finally drop the 'me.'

When I look 'here' I find I'm just spacious capacity for the world. I'm open, non-judgmental, colorless, peaceful and all loving. As are you!

LOOK AT YOURSELF

How we appear in the world depends on where we are observing ourselves from. This relativistic perspective was key to Douglas Harding's philosophy and is explained perfectly By Richard Lang in his wonderful book "Seeing Who You Really Are."

To summarize, from 6ft, I'm a person, a man of middle age with blonde hair and a twinkle in my blue eyes. If you move closer, then from 6 inches I'm a face, some skin and hair. Moving in closer to within a few millimeters you can see my pores and hair follicles. Moving in closer still you can see my cells. Moving yet closer you can see that these cells are made up of a nucleus and a sea of molecules. Moving in even closer you can see that the molecules are made up of atoms. Moving closer you can see that these atoms are made of electrons, protons and neutrons. Moving closer we can see that our atomic particles are made up of an array of sub-atomic particles and nobody know where it all stops!

At this distance, we can see that far from being solid, atoms are almost entirely composed of empty space. The sub atomic world is more like a solar system in terms of the mix of matter verses space than anything we would normally think of as solid.

It turns out, no matter how close I zoom in I'm unable to reveal what's behind me, what's the physical basis of me at zero distance. At the limits of our knowledge there is almost nothing, just space, your solidity at 6 inches is revealed to be an illusion at the atomic and sub atomic levels where you are almost entirely empty space. At center, you are an unknowable mystery. You are a bubbling effervescent nothing.

Moving away I can see I'm on a train (again) and I'm just pulling out of Euston Station, which is in London, which is in England, in Great Britain, in Europe which is on the earth, in the solar system, in the Milky Way, in our Universe which is perhaps part of a multi-verse and who knows what.

Each perspective has its own emergent properties. I'm not any one of these perspectives, I'm all of them. You might not normally identify yourself with the planet or solar system, proteins and atoms but you depend on all these layers. Take away any one of them and we can't survive. You are not separate from these.

All views are relative and have relative properties. I'm none of these. I'm the unchangeable essence of which these are just views, and the nature of the view depends on the position of the viewer. These views tell us more about the perspective of the viewer not about the viewed.

I have a human face, a planetary face, a universal face, an atomic face and a molecular face. However, none of these are my reality. These faces are relative to the position of the viewer. My reality is that I am the empty knowing space for all, as are you!

AWARENESS, AWARENESS, AWARENESS

There is only awareness. Consider the objects of awareness. Consider thoughts, consider feelings, emotions, sounds, images and smells. Consider what they are made of.

Just like in the ocean, ask what the waves, currents and whirl pools are made of. They are all modulations of the ocean. In the same way, all objects in awareness are modulations of awareness. There is only awareness. We know our thoughts through awareness. Of course, there are times when we are not aware of awareness. Indeed, many if not most people are rarely if ever aware of awareness.

The way it works, is that the objects within awareness modulate awareness; but they don't change it. In its primacy awareness remains aware and pristine. A tidal wave might race across the ocean, but the ocean remains the ocean.

PRISTINE, UNCHANGING, AGELESS, DEATHLESS

Consider the TV screen, it starts blank, then takes on the colors and brightness of the images it displays. The TV Screen remains a screen, but its appearance changes. The TV screen goes from blank to a bright sequence of moving images, then when it's turned off it goes back to blank. The TV Screen is totally unaffected by the image it displayed moments before.

The awareness you had as a ten-year-old is the same awareness that you have at forty and just as pristine at ninety.

UNIVERSAL AWARENESS

Awareness is not personal; this awareness I have is the same awareness you have. The exact same. It's the same awareness that Hitler had, the same as Mother Theresa, the same as Albert Einstein and the same as Jesus or Buddha. The exact same awareness, not similar!

The difference is mostly the degree to which we are aware of awareness. That is all evil, genius and divinity is. That is all love is. That is all that sets you apart from Jesus or Buddha, just the simple knowing of knowing.

CREATION

Following our ocean analogy, we can say that the ocean is modulated by the environment, by gravity, by the heating of the sun and by a myriad of geological processes. Awareness however, is modulated by what 'is' and it is modulated into 'what is.' However, awareness's source is not the environment, its source is the void. Out of nothing comes all! When things pass from awareness they return to the void. Back to nothing all must go! Eternal birth, eternal death, destiny is unstoppable.

WHO DO YOU REALLY WANT TO BE?

WHAT DO YOU WANT?

I'M SURE YOU'VE given what you want, quite a lot of thought over the years. I've wanted so many things. However, as I look back at my life, I see that my wants as I experienced them were detached from my true life's purpose. My plans didn't connect or lead to what I was really yearning for from my heart.

I wanted the toy, the friend, the girl, the job, another job, a house, a car, a smarter car, a bigger house, to make my wife happy, a job that wasn't killing me and I guess you've had a similar pattern of wants.

As we discussed earlier, none of these things fill the gap that I felt in my life and you've probably come to a similar understanding about your life too.

Do you want to keep on wanting more, or are you ready for a deeper awareness to fill that void? Are you ready to be satisfied, to be complete to be whole?

WHERE DO YOU WANT TO BE?

In my formative years, my aspirations were always out in front of me. My pressing desire was to be away from where I was. Never, did I just want to be exactly where I was, or for everything to be as it 'is'.

Each time I was where I'd imagined I'd wanted to be, I wasn't there. Even when I was on holiday sitting in Kostas restaurant on the Greek isle of Agistri, I wasn't there. Rather than savor the moment, savoring the sunset, savoring the food, savoring the sun warming my skin, savoring the banter with the waiter or just savoring time spent with my wife. I would be thinking of taking a photo, so I could remember the moment later. At moments, I was thinking about who else would love it here, rather than simply loving here, loving it right now as it is. At other times, I was thinking about where to go next and what that would be like.

You can see how my attitudes of the future and past have robbed me of the now. You can understand how your attitude to the future and past has so often robbed you of the 'now' and is continuing to take you away from the moment.

HOW DO YOU WANT TO BE?

There's great guidance to be found in how you really want to be. You must ask yourself the question, "What do I want my life to be like?"

You must look behind the answers to the deeper truth.

In my early career, I wanted to be successful, wealthy and in control. When I looked behind that story what I saw was the deeper truth. What I saw was the 'why' behind my first level of aspiration. What I saw was that I wanted to be peaceful, happy, content, free from struggle, and at ease in the world.

Looking back, it's clear that being successful, wealthy and in control are not real ends, and the things I was doing would never give me the life I really wanted.

Take some time now to understand or reflect on how it is you want to be. If you can identify your primary aims, you can use these as a compass to navigate your life and keep moving in harmony with your purpose.

UNCOVER YOUR PRIMARY AIMS

Before reading further, take some time now to understand and reflect on how it is you want to be. As you prepare to take your next steps in life, as you prepare to start a new project, be aware if the things you are doing or plan to do are moving you towards these aims or away from them.

Ask yourself. "Are my goals, projects and day to day activities consistent with my primary aims?"

To help you I've prepared a series of questions. Just, read the question and answer with your gut instinct, this will probably be the first thing that comes into your mind:

1. What things do I value most e.g. health, family, time, etc.?

2. What kind of life do I want e.g. happy, exciting, calm, secure, etc.?

3. What do I want my life to look like e.g. ordered, calm, pleasant, etc.?

4. Who do I wish to be in the world at large e.g. a good husband, a mother, a father, a friend, a wife, boss, etc.?

5. What do I wish my life to be like on a day-to-day basis e.g. orderly, productive, and fulfilling?

6. How would I like to be with others e.g. understanding, supportive, helpful, interesting, etc.?

7. What would I like to be doing in: 1, 2, 3, 5, 10 or 20 Years e.g. interests, work, income, holidays, home, etc.?

8. What do I want to learn in my life time e.g. at work, academically, etc.?

9. How much money do I need to live the life I'm thinking of?

You might not have been expecting the more material questions but earning money and work are important part of life and knowing how much money you need is a good starting point because not having enough can be a distraction to say the least!

There's no time like the present. Write up your responses to these questions now.

When you've completed the primary aims, leave it for a day or two then read it and see if you're happy with your answers. Meditate on your answers.

Ask yourself: Why did I say what I've written? Who would be most pleased by this? Is there a hidden agenda behind any of my answers?

BEING UNSETTLED IS GOOD

When you look at your primary aims there are probably few surprises, but when you look at how your life is now you might find there's quite a big disconnect between how your life is and what your primary aims say you want your life to be.

Those uneasy thoughts are not bad, seen from another point of view they are your salvation. If you observe these thoughts, they will tell you you're going the wrong way. All you need to know is that feeling that you're going the wrong way, then you know enough. If you pay attention, these feelings can direct you back in the right direction.

For example, you might be saying that peace and love are important but at work you're constantly in conflict and feel unloved. When you look at where your current life is taking you, you might realize that it's not going to meet many of your primary aims.

Guess what? If your current plan isn't meeting your primary aims, it's time to get a new plan or at least change your plan into one that will meet your aims.

If you're feeling uneasy, that's great, that's awareness that you're going off the path. Yesterday, you may well have felt this same unease about what is happening. However, now you know why you've felt this sense of angst about your life. You don't feel angst any more you feel a call to awareness and you pay attention to what it is telling you. Not this, not this!

It's important to act on these feelings of discontentment or ill-ease because if unattended this dis-ease will manifest in your life as physical disease.

Primary aims are not in themselves the answer or the way, but they are good pointers and barriers that can keep you on track.

Primary aims are also a great source of inspiration to face where you are and see it with clear eyes and find the motivation to do something else. They also provide you with a useful meditation on your motives and values.

Don't be afraid to change your aims as you progress on your path. Be afraid to live a life that is not aligned. This is no life it's an existence.

INSIGHT ON THE ROAD TO YOUR PURPOSE

As I came to know my primary aims, I started to move along an ever more harmonious path, I was drawn towards many lessons and this helped me to connect to life in much deeper ways of being.

Now my greatest aspiration is this, right now as it is, to simply love life as it is, to be openness for life and enjoy oneness with all.

In time, you will come to rely less on your primary aims. Initially they may evolve for a while but in the end, they will melt away. What you will trust is the universe and your sense of alignment to its purpose.

Remember though you are not your primary aims, these are of the "me" and not the "I", these are part of the story you have of you. Getting them out in the open helps you to live authentically exactly because you know what they are, and because you know you are not that.

THE ANSWER TO "WHO AM I?"

Douglas Harding has many revelations to offer us but all of them are an extension of his hypothesis, which was his answer to the question of who you really are. This is the question many mystics down the ages have posed, "Who am I?"

Douglas's hypothesis is that you are not what you look like.

> *"Though you appear to others (at a distance) as a unique person, to yourself (at no distance), you are boundless and timeless emptiness – awake space that is capacity for the world."*
>
> *Douglas Harding*

Douglas was a practical man and not content with anything abstract he dedicated his life to giving people the tools and the encouragement to experience themselves at center. He wanted people to experience themselves as the 'I' that 'I Am'. He was deeply concerned that people needed to look for themselves and when looking, should discard what is not there, discarding what is not seen.

In this sense, Douglas's hypothesis harks back to empirical philosophy, which is concerned exclusively with what can be observed. To this he adds a relativistic twist.

However, unlike most of science, which is conducted from the third person, where the scientist is removed from the object being observed, separate. Douglas is observing from the first-person, he is the subject and never removed from what is being observed.

This is refreshing when compared to 'New Age' or religious beliefs which are unscientific and shy away from any sort of challenge or testing.

The insight that you gain when you look for yourself is to realize that you are not as unique as you appear. From zero distance, we are all the same. True, but only you can know your experience of this oneness and for this reason you must look for yourself. Moving forwards, only you can discard what is not there, only you can discard what you have added!

When you look out at the world from your center, you start to see that you are behind all your troubles, or perhaps more accurately you are in front of all your troubles obscuring the truth and then in awareness you can see past them all.

The point is that when you become zero-centric rather than ego-centric you don't have to suffer all the troubles, they are not part of you. You can see them, then suddenly they are no longer the lens through which you see the world. They are no longer what you are bringing to the world. Instead, all your troubles are exactly what they are, just thoughts that are drifting through your consciousness. However, now you can watch your thoughts instead of living them, or more particularly, rather than being 'lived by' your thoughts!

Oh, dear reader, if you will only come to this core, all your troubles will start to drop away. Then in awareness you can get on with doing exactly what you must do. You can organize your debts, open your business, do the accounts, and plan a wedding. You can do it all from a place of peace, without the drama and with a fraction of the energy or time it took you before. Not only will you get it all done, but each task will be a source of joy.

GETTING HOME IS SIMPLE

What Douglas Harding has achieved is a monumental achievement. He has made this core experience, what Douglas playfully called being zero-centric, available to anyone.

Together with a host of seeing friends he devised a multitude of simple tools or experiments as Douglas liked to call them. These exercises enable people to get zero-centric and explore this inner landscape for themselves. We will use a few of these tools later so that you can experience zero-centricity for yourself.

WHAT WILL YOU EXPERIENCE AT ZERO DISTANCE?

When we look inside and then look out from this core we discover the place where 'I' is truly looking from.

What we find is that it all fits in, we find that we are capacity for everything, nothing is outside of this capacity. Nothing is too big, nothing is too ugly, nothing is too beautiful, nothing is repulsive, nothing is too distant, and nothing is too precious. Our center has no ends or edges. It has no color or texture of its own but embraces all. We discover that this is the 'I' that I am.

At zero distance this is all I am. I'm no-thing and nothing troubles me, and nothing leaves any stains on this space that I am.

At my center, I'm like a mirror that reflects whatever object is before it and when the object is removed just like a mirror the object leaves no trace on who I am. Like the mirror I accept all, nothing is judged, nothing is required everything is perfect as am I.

I'm aware space and no one is outside of my being, we are all together in oneness. The legacy of this vision of what we are at our core, is the awareness that follows in its wake. We start to see you as me and me as you, loneliness becomes a non-sense and fear falls away in the light of this beatific vision of true love.

When I come to the center, I'm left in awe at what I am and what you are. At center, I'm peaceful, content and aware. But there's more!

THE PHENOMENA OF ME

As I said earlier, most of us clearly don't see the world from our center, we are a little removed and see the world from what I have been calling 'Me' and you have been looking from what you'd call 'Me' too.

To locate me, bring your hand to your face, feel it, that's the 'you' that is your 'Me.' 'Me' is what you project out into the world, it is part of the world and when you look from 'I' at center you see 'me' is just another object, of the world and in the world.

This 'Me' phenomena is the main obstacle to living and being as you are. It's this 'Me', the story, which is keeping you from a life of peace, love and happiness. You created 'Me' and in doing so you 'thing' this 'No-Thing' you are insane in your attempts to make an object out of the ultimate subject. Inadvertently, you are trying to cork the genie back into the bottle.

It's in 'Me' that you'll find all your beliefs and all your crazy dreams, and it's these beliefs that twist what you see around your judgments. In contrast to 'I', 'Me' is no mirror. In fact, the 'Me' is constantly disturbed by the objects before it. However, a mirror is what you truly are. You are the universal mirror.

ME TIME

Over time 'Me' succumbs to time, the youthful face dies and wrinkles, the 'Me' is corrupted by the passing years until the body finally falls away into total decay.

Whereas the 'I' is immutable, changeless, deathless. The capacity is the same at 6, 16, 66 and 96. It's the same capacity as it was 2600 years back, or 2000 years back or 1400 years back.

ARE YOU READY?

We've been flirting with a new mystic way of being. I've tempted you with the possibility of dropping your old ego-centric self, of leaving all seeking behind and I alluded to the possibility of coming home to who you are at center. Where you will find peace, happiness and contentment.

Words come cheap, and if I had $1 for each person that has read book after book but never paused for long enough to put any of the insights into practice, well, I'd be rolling in it, I'd be able to buy a Caribbean Island and why not!

The point of this book is not to explain things, or name things or even to make you aware of yourself and your purpose in life. The book is in your hand now so that you can practice what I'm going to show you, not learn it. It's not here just so you can while away a few hours in my company. The 'Way Within' is not about more learning. The 'Way Within' is about experiencing what 'is' as 'it is'.

Please, if anything I've said resonates with you, then as you read the rest of the book take the time to do each exercise for yourself. Not once but many times. Don't move on until you've done each exercise and if that means you put down the book, put it down. Don't read on until you've tried the latest exercise you've read. As you move through the book keep going back to the earlier exercises, keep looking at what you find, take it as it is all the time trying to see free of all your life experiences, knowledge and beliefs.

You will benefit if you can find some other seekers to practice with and share notes with as we all benefit from company along the way. But don't dwell on it or worry if you must travel alone, such is your path for now! From what I hear and from what I have experienced, the path generally brings you all the company that you'll ever need. The thing is to get going and keep going.

MEETUPS

I would strongly urge you to seek out likeminded people. The best way is to check out www.meetup.com and search for key words like "Non-Duality", "Spiritual Book Group" or maybe one day "The Way Within" or even "James Capra".

If you can't find one, then why not start your own? Feel free to reach out to me and I'll help with materials, set up and even join you via dial in, video conference or if I'm in town I'd love to come in person.

AWE AND PEACE

After we start to see we are increasingly full of awe. Later, as we awaken to our sage will, we are filled with peace. As a sage, the awe is still there, but it is balanced by a new calm. The knowledge that "All is well, and all shall be well" emerges from the new vision and fills your cup.

As a seer, you look past your problems to the truth. As a sage, there are no problems, just awareness. You are awareness and no thoughts can touch you now, nothing can corrupt you when you are the mirror of the world instead of its victim.

Moving beyond seeing will happen quite quickly once you start seeing.

THE PROBLEM OF GOOD AND EVIL

So, what is evil? Where does evil come from? Why do we have evil? People are often asking these sorts of questions.

If I am that which is unchangeable, open to all. If I am that which contains all, and intends all, then doesn't that raise questions like, "Am I not evil too? Am I not open to evil? Should I not embrace evil?"

These are questions that seekers sometimes struggle with as they intellectualize their true nature. As essence, what we are referring to here as evil, is just a modulation of awareness. A modulation that can only arise when there is no belief in the oneness of all. Evil then is a product of unawareness. Evil is a current in the ocean of awareness.

In awareness there is no separation, no separate self to harm. There is just the ocean and we are all that. In awareness, we can never harm ourselves, so by extension we can never harm anyone or anything. This is the non-dual view, this is the enlightened view.

Don't get me wrong. If you come face to face with evil, don't be passive, don't run away into the peace within. Don't naively hide in that safe place within.

Likewise, don't try to reason with evil. Don't try to help its victims to understand the problem of evil from the point of view of awareness.

Act in the moment. Act with purpose. Do what is needed. Do it without attachment. Do it without judgement. Do it without anger or malice. Do it with love and presence.

Evil can never hurt or harm the 'I' but it can impair your progress towards an enlightened life. It can drag you into unawareness. It can inflict real damage, very real damage on the body. So, act. Move. Do what you must do.

Never engage evil. Never join it in hate. See it. Have compassion. Love it. See the child. Be the parent. This doesn't mean standing by, it doesn't mean letting the evil doer misbehave.

Love the evil doer as the wise parent loves the errant child.

When you drop the illusion of evil you are left with what 'is', and this is always love. Hear the call for love. The child before you is only ever calling for love, unaware love. This person's truth is the same as your truth. This person is you, they just don't know it. You are this person, be aware of it. This child's love is not given, it is twisted into what you now see. This is the call for love.

Be aware, this is no toddler before you this is a two-hundred-pound monster that probably won't recognize what he really needs even when he is given it. The illusion masks love with fear and scared people do crazy things. Don't be scared, but don't get too close either. This person is crazy.

So, evil is just unawareness, but what of Good?

Well, you must be careful there too as good is also just an illusion. Good is just a judgement of what 'is'.

Awareness and the aware person is not good. The saint is not good. The saint just is. People may judge the aware action as good, they may not, and any judgement is just their story. Their judgement is not the sages story, their judgement is nothing to do with you.

So, in a way, good and evil are the same problem for the seeker. Good and evil are a problem of judgement. Both good and evil are just products of the unaware mind.

For the aware, for the sage, there is no good and no evil. For the sage, there just 'is'. There is however, an absence or presence of awareness. The sage is open to this so that they can act exactly as the moment requires.

HOW DO YOU BECOME A SEER?

WHAT IS A SEER?

BEFORE WE GO further it's worth a quick re-cap. The hypothesis we have is that mostSpiritBrew people are seeking things. They are looking for their lives and the people and things around them to be somehow different.

The problem is that the answer to this search is not to be found out there in the world but by redirecting our attention inside and becoming aware of what we are at our center.

Experience is relative in that what you experience depends on how far you are from what is being observed. Seeing is about observing the world from zero distance, looking from your center, looking from the hub of the universe.

Seeing is looking at the world from the calm of our center and accepting what we see as it is without projecting our prejudice and judgements onto the world.

As a seer, we can see past the problems that occupied our lives as seekers, because as a seer these problems are not part of us and are visibly not real. From our center, they are just thoughts that are passing through our consciousness without changing a thing.

As a seeker, you're like the man who is trying to carpet the world.

As a sage, you are like his friend who just slips his slippers on and walks the world in comfort.

SEEING SHIFTS AWARENESS

An important aspect of becoming a seer is the realization that thoughts, feelings, things, the mind, and the body are all objects that appear in awareness.

This realization leads to the shift from knowing yourself as a mind, in a body that moves around an external world to understanding oneself as the aware spacious capacity in which all objects appear. Ultimately seeing that objects don't exist within this space like the stars you as a separate observer see in a big universe; they are made from the space, they are awareness. As are the stars! You are them too!

SEEING IS NOT A WAY

Seeing is the opening move in your pursuit of 'The Way Within', it is the first thing about you that will change, it will flip and as it flips so will you.

Seeing is really the easiest thing in the world, it's your natural state of mind with nothing added. As you see, you'll experience many paradoxes. The first and one of the most disturbing comes when you see that taking in the world, being open to all is your nature, it's the easiest thing because you are so wide open. However, and here's the paradox, part and parcel of this is that you'll end up not merely looking at it all, you'll quite literally take it all on, you'll take it on with all its guilt, pain and fear.

This consequence of seeing and its resolution, which is the next step along the 'Way Within' is more than we can take on in this book. Which is why I'll come back to it in my next book, where being it 'All' and loving it 'All' are key themes.

Try not to over think any of this for now, let it wash over you and take comfort when I tell you that awareness is the key and "All is well, and All shall be well, and all manner of things shall be well".

HOW DO YOU BECOME A SEER?

Becoming a seer is part and parcel of the natural evolution of awareness. To illustrate what I mean it helps to think of awareness as a series of stages that go from infant awareness to God awareness. The stages are:

Infant – See the world as it 'is'.

Child – Start to see the world through language.

Adult – See the world through your story and societies norms.

Seer – See the world again as it 'is' with awareness of what it is not.

Sage – Love the world as it 'is'.

God – Be the world as it 'is'.

Don't get attached to these stages, they just illustrate in words the nature of the progression. It won't be exactly like this for you. Your path is unique and reflects where you started from and all the baggage you're carrying. It also reflects how far you've travelled so far.

AWARENESS OF AN INFANT

As an infant during our first couple of years we see the world as it 'is'. The infant sees as-is because they haven't anything to put in the way of what 'is'. The infant relies totally on what is given. For the infant there is nothing, no 'me' in the way of what they are. Nothing in the way of where they are, or what they're doing. Everything is an infant's, there is no distance, and the moon is no further than the hand that tries to pluck it. The infant's world really is his world, distance hasn't snuck in and stolen it from him. For the infant, the obvious is the obvious, and when someone goes out of his room they cease to be.

The infant is like all animals, he is totally headless and unseparated from the world at large. The infant doesn't own the reflection that greets him in the mirror, the reflection stays where it was, it's not his, but some other infant over there.

For an infant, there is only 'now' and 'is'. All things appear out of the void and in time disappear back into no-thing.

AWARENESS OF A CHILD

After infanthood, we move into childhood. The transition from infant to child starts with the arrival of language and is achieved with language. His transformation is characterized by the forming of attachments, my car, my mum and with these attachments come early emotions and a sense of expectation of how things should be.

The infant sees a sparrow dancing on his window ledge and he's all full of wonder and awe. The infant is brimming with excitement and he rushes to tell his mummy about the little wonder dancing and singing on his window sill and mummy tells him it's just a sparrow. Next day the sparrow comes back and is spotted by the infant's playmate who's likewise infected with awe, but the rapidly maturing child now points out to his friend, that it's just a sparrow. This time as a child he doesn't see something magical and wonderful he just sees another sparrow. The infant is now a child. He now has a name for the wonderful sight, a label and suddenly a step is taken, and the child is removed from reality. The magic slips away word by word, label by label. The label becomes the child's reality.

After our innocence of infanthood, we have started to go out into the world and look back at ourselves and not just with our eyes we have started seeing through the eyes of others. We've started seeing this head on these shoulders and connected that face with me and answered to its name. But behind the head there's still spacious capacity and innocence but our attention is focusing more and more on our public face rather than our private space.

In the end, it is the child that pays the price of forgetting who we are in order that we can become human.

AWARENESS OF AN ADULT

As our awareness matures we become adults, but this follows no strict time-line. For some it happens before they become a teenager for others it's held off until much later in life. Harding sums up the journey to adulthood better than I ever could in "On Having No Head" when he says:

> *"We don't grow up, we grow down – instead of being present with the stars, and all things under the stars, we have shrunk away and withdrawn from them. Instead of containing our world, it now contains us or at least, what's*

*left of us. And so, reduced from being the whole
scene into being this tiny part, is it any wonder if we find ourselves in all sorts of trouble, if
we grow greedy, resentful, alienated, frightened,
defeated, tired, stiff, and imitative instead of
creative?"*

Douglas Harding

As adults, the truth is that our happiness is deep rooted and real,
whereas our misery is shallow rooted and unreal, born of delusion and
ignorance. We suffer because we overlook the fact, that at heart, we are
all right. We suffer because we imagine ourselves separate and short
lived when in truth we are at one with all and immortal. Overlooking
our true nature and that we are all right, we are constantly stressed. We
must cope with self-doubt, anxiety, loneliness, jealousy, boredom, fear,
death and guilt to name just a few of our adult feelings.

Adults must suffer as part of coping with our humanness.

PRIVATE AND PUBLIC SELF

There are two sides to our nature. First, there's the public, the self
that we put out in the world. This is the face the world sees and for
nearly all of us it is self-created, and it includes all the stories we keep
telling about who we are. In the world, I'm James. I'm this, I'm that
and I'm the other. This is the 'me' we talked about earlier. Critically,
this is more than just the face you have in the world, more than the
fiction you are creating, this 'me' is also the lens that you see the
world through.

The other side of our nature is our private self. This is the place
within that only we can experience. This is the spacious capacity, the
mirror on which the world, indeed the universe plays out. In character this space is the same for all, but only you can know your private
self for yourself moment by moment.

As a seer, we see from the center. We see from our private self
and from there we see our public self. However, as a seer, we don't
see through the public self, for the seer the public self isn't a lens that
changes what we see. We see our public self as just another object. As
a seer, you see past the public self not with it.

This is in stark contrast to most people whose private self is drowned out by the ego, which is the echo of the public self as the mind reflects on the world at large and how the 'me' is affected by past, present and future events that may or may not even happen.

AWARENESS AS A SEER

Those that turn their backs on looking out into the world, those that have given up 'what is not,' those that have been conscious for a moment and looked in to see what 'is', they have become seers.

All you must do is redirect the arrow of your attention. When your attention is redirected you become aware of yourself at center. You simultaneously experience your private self at zero distance and your public self at large in the world. As a seer, you can start to live aware of both your public and private self so that you can be appropriate for other's sake yet always aware.

This is the child that Jesus spoke of. The child we need to emulate if we are to enter the kingdom of heaven. An innocent, yet one that is aware of both their public and private faces. An innocent with a capacity that is open to all, not touched by anything but aware of all.

The seer no longer looks out with the body's two eyes, he is aware space, boundless capacity that is always open, and everything is taken into him. He has stopped moving in the world, now he is still, and the world moves within him.

AWARENESS OF THE SAGE

Seeing brings the opportunity to live the life of a sage. Living in the way, doesn't mean anything about what you do, but everything about how you do it.

A sage lives a life of love. Having seen what is, they live beyond what is not, without fear. For a sage, having removed fear, he is left with only love. A sage is left with only love, love of what 'is'. For a sage "All is well, and All shall be well, and all manner of things shall be well in the world".

The sage is beyond knowledge and lives a life of wisdom. The sage is totally at peace with life as it is. Sages don't have to live on a mountain top, they don't have to withdraw from life. If you think about it, it's easier to become a sage amid life. Whereas, it's impossible to be at peace if you have withdrawn from the world and left what you'd struggled to love behind. This isn't enlightened, it's limited not limitless.

For the most part, sages look, sound and work just like you do. It's just that they do it all in awareness and with wisdom. They don't do sage type stuff, they go to work, hail taxis, get the subway go to the theatre, wash their clothes do their shopping, they even pay their bills. Sometimes they even forget to pay their bills.

If a seer is someone that sees the world from their center with nothing added then a sage having seen, simply wants life, the universe and the moment to be just as it is. He fully accepts whatever happens as it happens. The sage goes further as he doesn't merely accept what is, he intends it.

THE TRAP OF RETREAT

For many there's a time after starting to see and after knowing ourselves as spacious capacity, when we falter. It's a trap and like all traps it doesn't feel like a trap. It feels like enlightened action! I for one became quite cold, the tears of the ones I loved didn't touch me, or the daily scenes of woe left me unmoved because I was acting as if I was the mirror which is only part of the story.

The trap arises when we separate the objects from ourselves as subject. Having seen ourselves as capacity, it's an easy step to see the objects that appear as being separate from us because they don't disturb us. It's a time when many of us retreat from the problems we see in the world into our new home. We retreat to the place where things come and go, and we remain unaffected. We artificially assume a distance that is just not there.

This is a subtle problem. The solution is to stop retreating from the world and stop dutifully accepting what 'is' because intellectually you've embraced acceptance as a principle or belief. This sort of acceptance is an act of blind faith. This sort of acceptance is the sort that comes second-hand, not first-hand, it doesn't come from direct first-person experience. Instead, it is important to accept what 'is' from an understanding that it's not just what you want, it is what you have willed to be. You are not merely host to all things you are an integral part of their creation.

When you love what 'is' you are no longer a mere mirror, though on one level you are untouched on another you are what 'is' and you have complete compassion and understanding for all because all is love.

AWARENESS OF GOD

Only when you let everything go, can you emerge into the awareness of God. It's not enough to take the next step, you can't make it happen. You must surrender to it and then it unfolds as and when it 'is'.

In oneness, you are beyond life and beyond death. You are the pulse of the eternal mind.

EACH STAGE IS A PLATEAU

I like to think about our journey through life as an ascending series of plateaus, with each plateau being defined or perhaps rather reflecting our current view of the world. In this way, we live on a level and we stay on that level coming up against the same problems. We keep making the same mistakes over and over until we get the lesson of this plateau. Once we get the lesson our world view changes and through this change of mind we ascend to or rather create the next level. With our next level of being comes a new set of problems, and we make new mistakes, until we finally get it and our perception changes again and we ascend to the next level.

There's never anything wrong with the world or what it provides us. It's just a matter of our false beliefs about the world and false beliefs about what happens. It is these false beliefs that we've been coming up against, and it's these beliefs that have caused all the problems.

Climbing the plateaus is really a matter of losing something rather than gaining anything. Each time, we lose a bit more of our ego, some of our false world view falls away, something that we've been adding to the world is left and leaves the world in peace. This is in stark contrast to how we've tried to progress our lives, where previously we've been trying to add something to ourselves. We've been trying to add something whether it was a new belief, a better body or new practices.

So, as we ascend, we increasingly find we are leaving the world as it 'is' without the need to add what 'is not' and as a result we find more peace, more love and bring more light into the world.

LIFE SERVES UP THE NEXT LESSON

Life brings the next issues that you need to overcome to your attention, you must be aware. Each problem is always a question of, what it is that you are adding to what 'is'. With awareness, it's easy to move upwards. These plateaus elevate you towards your home, to oneness and ever greater God awareness.

In other words, each plateau is just a lesson that needs to be learnt, something that needs to be dropped and you don't have to go looking for the lesson, it will be bugging you any moment.

NEITHER ACCIDENT OR DIVINE PLAN

I often hear people expressing how nothing is by accident and suggesting a universal intent in all things. I can't comment about that as I don't know. What I have observed, and observing is what I encourage you to do, is that when you look at the things that happen in your life, they reflect your views. They reflect the plateau you are on. From another perspective, they represent what is stopping you moving forwards.

Don't be surprised if what you need, and the right lessons show up in your life. We should be more surprised when neither appears because that's a clear sign that you're not paying attention.

What you project is exactly what you must let go of, it's the illusion of a fault in yourself that you must forgive, never a fault in someone else. There are no real faults, but there are plenty of illusions and plenty for you to let go of.

The challenge then is to keep your eyes open, listen, watch, don't judge and transformation will follow.

Alternatively, if you don't want to live as a seer with awareness, you can and will sleep walk your way through life and wait for crisis and death. This is your choice now. You are blessed because you have the freedom right now and every moment to choose. Most people don't get to choose, but another paradox is doing nothing is a choice and this is the path most people take. The sleep walker's way.

KEY ELEMENTS OF SEEING

There are many aspects to seeing, the following are the key universal qualities:

1. Seeing is the most accessible and obvious thing in the world. This is in direct contrast to what we've been told and have come to expect from the evolution of our consciousness.

2. Seeing is totally fool proof, when you turn your attention around and look at yourself from zero distance, then you can't fail to see. You may overlook the truth for a while but once you start seeing its revelation is inevitable.

3. Seeing has depth, indeed what you see is without ends. Try it now. Use your mind's eye, try to find a bottom of what you can see at center, look for end edge, look to find an end to it and you will find it has no bottom, no edges and no end.

4. What is seen by the seer is the same for all, this is not reserved for the sacred few. Our center is the same for all, it doesn't come in different hues or flavors, seeing is a universal constant, and a unifying principle.

5. Once you have experienced seeing what is seen is always on tap. It is never more than the width of a thought away and always in your gift to enjoy.

ATTENTION ON THE NOW

---- ❀ ----

DIRECTION OF ATTENTION

WE TOUCHED ON this earlier. Your attention can be directed into the space around you, it can be wandering back to past events, it can go meandering in the possible future or it can be inside other people's minds.

With the simple act of awareness, the focus of your attention becomes apparent and once you are aware mastery can follow.

There is a simple technique that you can use to help you switch the focus of your attention. It's called anchoring and it only takes a few moments to learn and will give you instant control over your attention.

AS we progress with the practices later in the book you can anchor yourself at center so that you can easily return get back to the peace and truth of who you are.

ANCHORING OUR ATTENTION

Before going further, I should recognize Paul Jones who writes about anchoring and other techniques in his wonderful book "How to live in the here and now." If you're not familiar with Paul and his work, I'd recommend a read.

For our purpose, we are only going to look at how you can anchor your attention in the present moment or Uptime as Paul likes to call it. Though as he illustrates you can anchor your attention to any of the potential directions of attention.

Don't dismiss the other possible directions of attention. All the directions of attention have their uses. For example, you can use anchors to switch your attention to the present, past, the future or to awareness of other people's minds. When needed this can be advantageous. Whereas randomly pondering other people's thinking, chewing other past mistakes or worrying about things that have not happened is rarely fruitful.

Although this chapter is about how to be a seer, and anchoring attention is not seeing, being able to return to the now at will and having awareness of when you are not present is a handy technique to cultivate and a powerful insight to have.

I'm also sharing this as anchoring was a very fruitful ingredient in my own spiritual development and it might prove as fruitful for you.

Once you have created an anchor that redirects your attention to the present moment, you can then use it to redirect your attention in an instant. All your fears and worries happen outside of the present moment, so being able to switch to the now is a powerful tonic for life.

Critically, the quality of your experience depends on the direction of your attention. The world is more alive, vibrant colorful and amazing when you're in the now. Clearly, it's useful and desirable to have a simple tool to make a more colorful life accessible as and when you want it.

There's nothing wrong with not being in the now. However, the quality of our moments, are significantly improved by being present and the likelihood of being a victim of our thoughts is removed.

The benefits are not just for you. You'll find that when you're in the now you are more attentive to what people are saying to you and no longer distracted by your thoughts about what they are going to say next. For the people we meet, this is a positive change. People can feel your attentiveness in a very deep way, they might not be able to put a finger on what it is about you, but they'll appreciate your attention and love.

Another thing that you may notice as you use this anchor is that your experience of space changes, as you start feeling space move through you, rather than the normal experience of you moving through space. For years, I used the anchor as I walked to work and loved the feeling of work coming to me. It is very peaceful and makes the whole experience of travel so much richer, engaging and pleasurable.

CREATING AN ANCHOR FOR THE NOW

The following is Paul Jones steps for creating an anchor to the present moment (uptime anchor). The anchor is produced by bringing your thumb and forefinger together while simultaneously experiencing the sensation of awareness in each of your senses. Through repetition the sensation of awareness becomes associated to the movement of bringing the thumb and forefinger together so that you can later rekindle your awareness by repeating the movement.

ANCHOR THE KINAESTHETIC SENSE

We will anchor your sense of feeling or 'body sense' first. This is what is known as the kinesthetic sense. We will have to repeat these steps for each of your senses. The other senses are your sense of smell and taste (Gustatory sense), hearing (Auditory) and sight (Visual).

Ready, there's no time like the present. Put your book down and do the following:

1. Relax and close your eyes. Send your attention into your body. Try not to verbalize your feelings, just become aware of raw sensations.

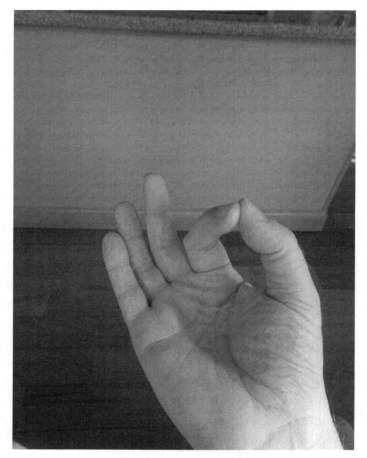

Figure 3 - Anchoring senses with thumb and forefinger

2. Once as much of your attention as possible is focused in your body squeeze the index finger and thumb of your right hand together to make a loop. This is your 'anchor', hold the anchor for a few moments or until you feel your concentration on your body wane or your concentration in general starts to drift away, then let your finger relax. Ideally, you'll relax your finger before your attention drifts.

3. Repeat this exercise several times. Each time use the thumb and forefinger of the right hand. The anchor will be made stronger by repetition.

ANCHOR THE GUSTATORY SENSE

Next repeat the anchoring steps but this time focus on your sense of smell and taste (Gustatory sense):

Pick something that has some taste and smell. You probably need to repeat for both smell and taste. I like to use gum for taste as I'm not tempted to swallow it and it keeps its flavor.

1. Relax and close your eyes. Send your attention into your taste buds and nose. Try not to verbalize your feelings, just become aware of the flavors or aroma.

2. Once as much of your attention as possible is focused on the taste or smell you are experiencing squeeze the index finger and thumb of your right hand together to make a loop. Hold the anchor for a few moments or until you feel your focus or concentration start to drift away, then let your finger relax. Ideally, you'll relax your finger before your attention drifts.

3. Repeat this exercise for some different tastes and smells several times and in no order. Each time use the thumb and forefinger of the right hand.

ANCHORING THE AUDITORY SENSE

Next repeat these steps for your sense of hearing (Auditory):

1. Relax and close your eyes. Send your attention into what can be heard. Try not to verbalize your feelings, just become aware of the sounds, picking out the foreground then exploring the background. Bring your attention on to each sound, maybe a bird song or police siren or some people talking in the distance.

2. Once as much of your attention as possible is focused on the sounds you can hear squeeze the index finger and thumb of your right hand together to make a loop. Hold the anchor for a few moments or until you feel your concentration drift in anyway, then let your finger relax. Ideally, you'll relax your finger before your attention drifts.

3. Repeat this exercise several times for a range of sounds. Each time use the thumb and forefinger of the right hand to anchor your attention.

ANCHORING THE VISUAL SENSE

Next repeat these steps for your sense of sight (Visual):

1. Relax and close your eyes. When you feel relaxed slowly open your eyes and take note of what you can see. Send your attention into what's being seen. Try not to verbalize your feelings, just become aware of what you can see.

2. Once as much of your attention as possible is focused on what you are seeing squeeze the index finger and thumb of your right hand together to make a loop. Hold the anchor for a few moments or until you feel your concentration start to drift away, then let your finger relax. Ideally, you'll relax your finger before your attention drifts.

3. Repeat this exercise several times and observe whatever you choose to look at. There are no right or wrong things to look at. The important thing is to associate the act of looking now with the anchor so that you can bring attention to what is being seen.

USING YOUR ANCHOR

After repeating the exercise several times for each sense, the anchor should be quite firmly established. You can now use your anchor any time you find your attention wandering or when you want to bring it sharply into focus apply the anchor.

Try it now. Wherever you are, right now, whatever you are doing bring your right thumb and forefinger together and your attention should be brought into the present moment and your senses engaged. You will find that the events of the moment and your natural bias to one or other sense will dominate where your attention lands. Your attention can't be focused on all senses at once, so don't expect that. In general, you like most people, will become aware of what is in your line of sight as sight is the dominant sense for most of us.

Personally, my anchor tends to bring attention to my body first then sight and gradually take in whatever sensations are stimulating my other senses.

Make this a practice to be used often and everywhere. It's amazing how this enriches your everyday experiences. You'll start to realize how little of your life has been conducted in awareness of the present moment. Suddenly, your walk to work will be a colorful and interesting experience where before it was lost to whatever train of thought was living you.

Through the now, you'll get your life back and you'll start living it in a much richer way. You'll also start to get a sense of when your thoughts are taking you out of the now and with the application of your anchor you'll be instantly resurrected to awareness of the now.

FROM 'ME' TO 'I'

THE SHORTEST JOURNEY

THE SHORTEST JOURNEY is the journey from 'me' over there, to 'I' here. Where are you now? Take a few moments right now to repeat the pointing exercise. What do you find at your center? Are you present, past or future? Are you elsewhere altogether? Are you wondering what it is that you experienced with the pointing finger? What are you now? Are you zero distance?

One glimpse of yourself won't transform your life, though it's all you need to seed the experience. If you want to receive all the benefits of what you truly are you need to go back, you need to get to know yourself at zero distance. You need to keep returning to that place we look out from, back to the listening silence that is our center. You need to keep going back to the no-thing that is aware of itself. Keep returning to this aware nothing, this spacious capacity that holds everything and judges nothing, the place that accepts all. Go back to the ultimate peace that is your heritage and your future, past and present.

Silence is not the absence of sound, but the absence of you. This is your journey, to drop 'you' not to find a peaceful place. Drop 'you' and you'll find peace!

If you haven't already repeated the pointing exercise do it now. Make the pointing exercise a daily practice. Try to weave it into your everyday routines and idle moments. Having said that, don't become a slave to it. I like to do it in the gym when I'm on the cross trainer. You might like to do it when you're waiting for someone to arrive or just before you go to bed at night. It doesn't matter where or when or with whom, though it's a good idea to mix up the when and where. The thing is to keep going back to your center to explore what you find there. When you're there, notice what you are, notice what you are not.

You're not what you've been projecting into the world, you're not any beliefs, you're not ego, and you're not angry, you're not judge or judged, you're not jealous, sick, happy or sad. You are certainly not a 'little you' deep down inside that is watching and controlling your environment through the body. There is no man inside the machine. Inside there is just space, infinite space.

EXPERIENCE ZERO DISTANCE

With a little practice, you won't need to keep repeating the pointing to center yourself, after a relatively short time you will find that you can direct your attention straight to your center. Take a moment now and see if you can redirect your attention to your center. Try to just experience yourself at zero distance.

Suddenly, as I redirect attention, I see my hands reaching for the keyboard and suddenly I'm no longer a thought! Suddenly, I'm no longer my stream of consciousness! Suddenly, I'm just awareness watching my hands at work, seeing my work and suddenly this page emerges before me.

From the center, I've stopped writing, writing is happening and I'm watching the book being written. Suddenly, it's not an effort on my part, my shoulders relax and my breathing slows and the quality of what is being written improves. I'm free, I'm not making it all happen and as I watch I'm struck with awe as these words emerge from the void. Wow, Oneness addressing Oneness. There's no me here, not my words. It's God talking to God. It's God talking to you, nothing to do with me.

YOU MAY BE DISSAPOINTED

The very ordinariness of seeing inevitably leads to us overlooking its wonder and power. At first glance or following initial exploration of yourself at center you might miss the value of what's before you. For many of us our true majesty remains masked by our own imagining and desires.

At this point, there's probably also still too much of you in the way. Perhaps you're still standing front and center totally blocking the view or perhaps you're just obscuring the view with your lingering presence. It's not just your ego or your imagination that's obscuring your ability to see clearly. There's usually some sort of preconceived idea about what things will be like when you become enlightened.

It's hard not to start to imagine what enlightenment is like, it's normal given all the hype to expect something special. Whereas, when you come home, what you come home to is the loss of all specialness, the absence of all difference, at center you come face to face with the most awe inspiring extra-ordinariness of is-ness, capacity and oneness.

It's so ordinary, so neutral, no flares, no rush, no sense of euphoria. Though things will probably start to appear brighter and more colorful. This is probably not what you'd been looking for. You've glimpsed it millions of times before, yet you totally overlooked it.

When you relax into what you see then amazing things start to happen. You will be in awe at what unfurls before your eyes and you will enjoy the greatest gifts imaginable.

WHAT WAS IT LIKE FOR ME?

The first time I did the pointing exercise I wasn't even under whelmed by the experience, as there really wasn't any experience to get. At the time, I was too busy trying to remember what to do, trying to get it right; while simultaneously, I was deeply worried that I was doing something wrong. I kept thinking that I was not worthy or perhaps not gifted enough to get it. With all that thinking going on, it's hardly surprising that I didn't see much. I was too busy worrying about the instructions, worrying that I was doing something wrong, worrying that I'd missed a vital instruction, thinking that I'm just not spiritual or good enough. I was consumed by my thoughts and the truth was obscured by a whirling mind of ideas, beliefs, doubts, fears and expectation.

The other problem was that I was convinced that I was on the trail of something that was somehow special. However, not only was what I saw and see now at center not special, it remained beyond me until with persistence I finally started to just take what I saw at zero distance at face value. It started to be clearer when I started taking note of what came into my awareness and started letting my bubbling imagination be, leaving my thoughts, which then started to fall away.

What I found was not what I'd imagined I was looking for. It was simply what I found, and it is this that I would like to direct your attention to. As it turned out, it was exactly what I need, and it is exactly what you need too!

One of my great gifts is my poor memory, so my memory of my first attempts to redirect my attention with the pointing exercise is quite vague. However, I know that I didn't really get it until I attended a workshop led by Richard Lang. In the workshop, it all made more sense, and Richard's direction took a whole load of responsibility away from my mind. The lesson is that it certainly took me a while and quite a few attempts to just accept what I was seeing. In contrast, I've attended workshops where friends have seen it immediately.

If it happens great, if not, don't be too hard on yourself. Try again, and again and each time try to just look without adding anything to what you are seeing. No memories, no beliefs, no expectations and no thoughts. Best of all join a group or attend a workshop.

If thoughts come to mind or memories crowd in, that's OK. Just observe them for a moment, observe them as if you were watching an ant cross a counter. This way, rather than a problem, your thoughts can be the keys to the kingdom as you become aware of the space into which your thoughts emerge, linger in and finally leave.

ASYMMETRY – GETTING 'FACE' TO 'NO FACE'

'FACE' TO 'NO FACE' – THE TUBE EXERCISE

THE TUBE IS a simple and often profound exercise. Unlike pointing you need a friend to do this. You'll also need a tube with a diameter that is roughly the same as the width of your face so that you can place your face in one end and look down the tube.

The idea of the tube exercise is that you place your face at the end and look toward the other end of the tube while a willing friend places their face at the far end of the tube so that you are looking down the tube at their dismembered face and they are looking at your face, which is similarly cut off from the rest of reality. The other person not only provides you with their face they are there to discuss the experience afterwards.

The tube can be made quite simply by rolling a piece of card into a tube and sticky taping it together or you can take a paper bag and cut out the bottom. You need enough light in the tube to be able to see so you may need to make some holes along one edge.

For me the exercise works best if you have a third person that can facilitate the exercise, giving direction and asking questions as you look through the tube. Being guided by a third person means that you don't have to give any thought to what happens next or what questions to ask. Having to think what to do next and give instructions can be a big distraction from the actual experience inside the tube.

The questions give you something specific to reflect on. Although having a third person is ideal, you can do the exercise with just two people. The best approach if you don't have a third person is to ask the questions one at a time and go into the tube after each question to reflect on your experience and what is seen. Play around with it and find out what works best for the two of you.

I find the questions help. When I first did the exercise, I was distracted by reflecting on myself, there was a lot of me in the tube. I was thinking things like, what do I look like today, is my breath ok, I hope there's not anything in my teeth, I hope I haven't got hairs coming out of my nose, etc. These thoughts took me away from the experience and into my ego self. Remember that the silence that we are looking for is the absence of 'me' not the absence of noise.

I find the following questions from Richard Lang's, "Seeing who you really are," are useful for facilitating the tube exercises:

1. On present evidence, how many faces do you see in the tube, one or two?

2. You can see a face at the far end, do you see your face at the near end?

3. Is your end of the tube wide-open?

4. Doesn't the time vanish into nothingness at your end, disappearing into clear, boundless consciousness?

5. How many clear, boundless consciousnesses do you see in the tube, two or one?

6. Is this single, undivided consciousness at the near end separate from the face at the far end?

7. Is there a dividing line between this space and that face?

8. As this space, are you built open for your friend?

9. Are you face there, to 'no face' here?

10. Having no face of your own, couldn't you say that your friend's face is yours?

11. In contrast to what you thought before, have you always been 'face' to 'no-face' with others?

REFLECTIONS ON THE EXPERIENCE

When you come out of the tube at the end spend a few minutes reflecting on the experience. Take turns to share what you saw, felt and thought. The dynamic is clear as we each have a slightly different perspective and diving into each other's experience enriches our own.

I think when we reflect on our experience in the tube at an absolute level we all have the same experience of 'face' there, to 'no face' here.

I'm talking about the level of what I call facticity. At this level, you're only concerned with what you see. When you 'see' you realize that what's really there is non-emotional. Seeing that I'm 'no-face' here and 'face' there is not dependent on emotions, I have emotions and my thoughts come and go. However, the fact is that I'm 'face' there and 'no face' here.

In our discussion of the experience in the tube we normally start with the feeling and thoughts the experience generates. Often as the discussion progresses we start to grasp the absolute that is behind it all.

In the tube, I'm totally open to you. However, when I reflect on my life, being open is not how I've been.

It occurs to me that I've lived as if there's a face here and a face there, I treat people as if they are behind the face there and I've acted as if I'm the face here.

Most of the time my behavior sub-consciously communicates my prejudice to the people I meet. I've spent most of my life as I'm sure most of you have playing what Douglas Harding called the 'face game'.

SWAPPING THE FACE GAME FOR OPENNESS

After years of playing the 'face game', when I finally see who I am from zero distance, I also instantly see who you are too. The space here, at my center, is the oneness that is in all.

When we see who we truly are we lose our appetite for the 'face game', because we now know that we are all faceless. We are not closed to each other, we are not in opposition. No, what I now see is that we are both totally open at our center. There is no opposition in awareness, I'm you and you are me. There's no wanting 'this' for me and 'that' for you. There's just acceptance of what 'is' and acceptance for whatever shows up.

The 'face game' is not a game that's worth playing, it's not much fun and there are no winners. Fortunately, once you start to see through the 'face game' it becomes much easier to stop playing it and to start being authentic. Being authentic is no game and unlike the 'face game' there are only winners.

Whether I am 'face' to 'no face' with another person that is aware of their facelessness. Or someone that is totally unaware is of no significance to me. Someone else's wakefulness is of no consequence to my state of mind exactly because it doesn't change my awareness.

However, I must say that being 'face' to 'no-face' ignites my humanity. There is something beautiful about loving someone and being totally open to the love that flow through us all.

Happiness is loving someone, loving anyone as they are, regardless of whether they are aware or not. This is seeing the world with Christ's eyes. Loving someone as they are, loving what 'is', seeing with Christ's eyes, this is the greatest blessing you can receive. There is no greater blessing!

LESSONS FROM THE TUBE

There's an important lesson about stress and personal relations that can be extracted from inside the tube. The tube experience reveals that we don't have any real stress in any personal or social relationships because we didn't have a relationship in the way that we'd imagined.

When we looked inside the tube we came to see how at this end of the tube it was always 'I' a spacious capacity, a 'no-thing', and as you know 'nothing' cannot be stressed.

At this end, there is nothing to be gained or lost, there's no confrontation. There is in fact 'nothing' to do the worrying and when we drop our thoughts there's nothing at either end of the tube to worry about.

How different this is from our experience outside the tube. How different it is for most of our life. Look around, you won't have to go far to see people that are face to face, the stress is palpable, and confrontations run on stress. Everyone is jostling, knocking one another. Just like on the underground railway that I take across London most days. I'm sure you don't need to go far to find the stress that I'm talking about.

In this chaos, there is a perfect symmetry as each opposing force meets its rival. However, this symmetry ends at this end of the tube where instead of trying to maintain a distance from the objects we face we see how we are empty space, perfectly asymmetrical so that we can take it all in. We are colorless for the colors, silent for the sounds, hungry for the taste of all that's before us. Nothing could be less stressful than being here for it all, being open.

PEACE IS BEYOND STRESS

The big insight is that at the heart of all the stress is peace. Once you come out of the tube, you need to remember to take on the stresses of the world, take it on 'face' to your 'no face', take it on as openness and with love not closed and in confrontation.

You can suddenly see that stress isn't something you have to fight. Instead stress is something you just correctly locate. You deal with stress by leaving it to be present where it is, over there. In other words, it's absent where it's not, which is right here where you are.

All the time you live consciously, from your center, you are free of all the stress. You are free from all stress if you are living from the unstressed here.

Your salvation comes when you see that you're not built for confrontation, you are no war monger because you are open to all and you have nothing to defend or defend against.

The way through stress is not about avoidance, it's never about running away from the stresses of life. Salvation comes when you stop running away from the stress, when you drop your face and embrace your no-face. Salvation comes when you dwell in your openness, when you dive into life and let it all flow through you.

STILLNESS AND SYMMETRY

---- ❦ ----

IMPLICATIONS OF SPACIOUSNESS

IF I'VE DONE my job well you should have come to an understanding that at center we are all spacious capacity for life, that we are aware no-thingness. This insight has many implications for life and particularly for how we make sense of the world.

In this chapter, we are going to think about what it means for your understanding of motion and stillness. We will also look at what your true nature must be for you to accommodate all.

ALL THINGS ARE IN MOTION

Things move, they never stop for a moment and their movements are, depending on your perspective, simultaneously gentle, swift, erratic and every point in-between.

To understand what I'm talking about we'll consider the empire state building. From 5th Avenue, the Empire State is clearly not moving an inch, but from geo-stationary orbit we can see that, due to the earth's rotation on its axis, that it's moving at about 1000 miles per hour. Step back further and we can see that the buildings planetary rotation is a trifle when compared to the speed at which it orbits the sun. From here the Empire State building is moving at

67,000 mph or 50 km per second.

Stepping back further we can see how the solar system is itself, is flying through space and by extension our little building, is speeding at 483,000 mph across our galaxy. Step back further and we can see how the galaxy itself if moving within the universe. This all adds up to a lot of speed and a very erratic course of movements through absolute space.

Step back further to the edge of the perceivable universe our galaxy is accelerating towards the speed of light. For these most distant observers the Empire State building accelerates until it reaches the speed of light and disappears forever beyond the edge of what can be perceived by these observers.

This festival of speed is true for all things everywhere, and it's been true since the beginning of time and so it must remain until it all ends.

Things move, and it appears that they are built from motion. It appears that things are made solid from motion. In contrast, you as capacity for life, as no-thing have neither internal nor external movement. You are stillness built of stillness.

MOVING HAND EXERCISE

This is one of the simplest exercises, all you need to do is make fist with your hand, either hand is fine. Then looking at it, shake it as quickly as you can.

What can you see? Does the hand blur with motion and time into a bigger thing, not quite as solid as the hand, but occupying a larger space?

It's a bit like when as a child when you whirled a sparkler round and round and made a circle of light. Just like the circle of light if you stop the motion or stop time the thing is 'un-thinged'. Suddenly, the stress is gone and in stillness we find the death of the thing. This is seen from the immortality of you as no-thing.

At the atomic level when we look we find the solidity of the world is produced by the motion within all the atoms. The atoms themselves are solid because their constituent particles are moving at speed. If you stopped an atom's electrons from spinning they'd collapse and the atom would cease to be. The atom would cease to be an atom. The atom would cease to be anything.

NOTHING IS STILL

We have been nurtured in the belief that we are things in the world interacting with other things as we move around the world. However, if we accept what we have seen for ourselves as we did the exercises, then we must accept that we are just spacious capacity for life.

If we embrace ourselves as capacity then it makes no sense to think of ourselves as objects in space, objects moving through space. Our old view of us as objects moving around space no longer makes sense when we are the space. As the space, we cannot move an inch as all inches are within us.

Space has different qualities from the objects it contains. It's not another mere container. Space as a container would be just another object, but this is not the case. Space is the subject, the 'I' not an object. It is first-person singular, not second or 3rd person plural.

I am nothing, I am still, and I am space.

Look inside and see the stillness, the space and see how the center of all this, the only true universal hub, the point at which you've been pointing at is no ordinary point. It's all points, it's a singularity. You are a singularity.

As awareness of your truth grows, the thing that you were in the world becomes still, motionless it dies. Your new awareness starts a chain reaction, a massive implosion that makes an atomic bomb seem like a puff of smoke. You are a black hole. Yet unlike the black holes in space, you give of a special light. The light of awareness!

THE LAW OF OPPOSITES

This is liberating, because as you are, you no longer chase around after things. All things are in you. What's more, not only do you not rush around, you don't imitate things. You are free of what you experience, you don't chase or copy. All things come to you, nothing touches you.

It's the nature of things, that you are the opposite of what you are currently occupied with. This is also known as the law of opposites. Though it's not like the opposites we encounter in everyday life, the relative opposites. It's not like cold being the opposite of hot, left being the opposite of right. The law of opposites is about being the complete absence of something so that it can be accommodated, so it can exist.

Cold isn't the complete absence of heat, cold is not the absence of heat that allows hot, it's just less hot. This is about being the complete absence of something so that it can exist.

The law of opposites is also known as the law of freedom from experience. This is the essence of your true nature as no-thing.

SYMMETRY OF NOTHING

I'm looking at my hands as I type and at center I'm emptiness for this scene. I'm colorless to take in the color of my hands, the keyboard, desk and screen. I'm stillness to take in the motion. I'm silence that births those key taps.

You are the stillness that takes in all motion, the silence from which all sounds emerge, the colorlessness that gives birth to the rainbow, the tastelessness and scentlessness that makes all taste and smell possible.

Silence is not the absence of sound, but the absence of you. It's the silence which gives the sound life.

Experience is born from this asymmetry of your nothingness and 'others' some-thingness. The perfect marriage of opposites, the juxta-position of absence and substance!

This law of opposites is at the heart of creation and it requires your absolute stillness to make all motion possible.

You are the no-thing that births all things. You are the silence from which birds sing.

BEING NOTHING

Something magical happens when you re-occupy your center. The magic starts when you come home and know yourself and live from your center as you truly are. People often talk about things seeming brighter, lighter and crispers as awareness grows in them. When you come home something truly profound happens that goes way be-yond these mere improvements in contrast.

As capacity, you totally become what you attend. To know what I mean, listen to Beethoven or Mozart from center. Listen as silence.

Suddenly, you are no longer hearing music, in your absence you become the music. It doesn't merely inspire a feeling in you, you are the feeling.

Don't think this being is reserved for such high moments at LV's glorious 5th. No, no, no, it is your nature to be everything. As I walk from the train I'm the beggar looking for spare change, the taxi driver waiting for his fare, the pigeon waiting for a scrap to be dropped, then I'm a swallow flying in formation, then I'm at my door and then I'm the door too as I yield to myself as the key.

I Am That I Am!

SELF-CENTER

One of the major causes of stress in our lives is our tendency to insist on our being something in the world. Our constant labelling of ourselves is onerous, deceptive and counterproductive.

The shift we need is from being an insanely ego-centered 'me' to a wholesome self-centered 'I'. The shift is from being an egotistic endeavor, it's the shift from being a self-created fiction, to embracing what 'is'. It's a shift from the ego's attempt to make the 'me'. A shift away from all the ego's efforts to make the person we present to the world.

All this effort to be something in the world, this effort to make our story into the hub of the universe is exhausting and ultimately impossible. The task the ego sets you is to centralize the peripheral, to make the 'you' that is forever removed from the center into the hub. Our ego-centricity is an endless task that quickly becomes a major source of frustration and stress.

Whereas living at center, living as center is the most peaceful, sustaining, stress free and positive thing you can do. Being truly self-centered is the surest cure for stress, fear and unhappiness. This is a pretty compelling motivation to jump the last few inches away from where you are 'not', to discover your center, where you always have been. Motivation to jump to reach the only true peace and stillness you will ever find no matter how hard or how long you seek.

It's ironic that we see it as being hard or even impossible when in fact it's a journey of no distance. All that separates you from this Nirvana is a thought, and how wide is a thought?

CENTER OF THE UNIVERSE

Ignoring that you are the center of the universe is a natural consequence of following what you've been told. It's a consequence of ignoring what you experience if you will only look for yourself. Almost no one looks because they have all the facts, if they do get a glimpse of the truth they ignore it, it's more convenient! The mind makes ignoring anything that contradicts its beliefs a way of life.

Your plight is confirmed because Science can find no center for the universe.

This lack of an official center allows you to declare any point as the center and the universal. Nature being what it is, you'll find all things conveniently arranged around this hub like paparazzi swarming around an errant celebrity. However, we're not declaring just any point the center. We're declaring center as the one spot that can never be caught off center, the spot you always occupy without occupying it at all.

UNTHING YOURSELF

If you are comfortable with your nature as capacity and 'nothing', then it's time to start to 'un-thing' yourself. Just now everything should be pointing at you your 'no-thing' nature. Everything is shouting out that you are the 'no-thing' that is the space for all things.

It's time to move from understanding to wisdom. It's time to stop resisting your uniqueness and your role in the universe.

I earlier raised the necessity to un-thing yourself, and of itself this 'un-thing-ing' will start to happen because it is in any case a natural consequence of taking your path. If you embrace the 'Way Within', this 'un-thing-ing' and the journey to true self-centeredness will be the next phase in your life journey.

THE SPINNING FINGER EXERCISE

I also like to call this the 'What Moves Exercise'. It helps to do this with a friend so that they can read the questions. Failing that you can always do it alone but if you're like me and blessed with a pitiful short-term memory it's quite hard to remember the words and do the exercise all at once.

If you do it on your own, don't get too caught up with the words. It's what you observe that counts.

Spinning the world needs nothing just your time and willingness to give it a go and a willingness to examine what your see. This exercise is a great way to get a sense that the world moves through you rather than the regular experience that you move through the world.

The procedure couldn't be simpler. You start by bringing yourself to center. If you have anchored your center use your anchor, if you can manage to center yourself by simply directing your attention to your spacious capacity that's wonderful, if not try doing the pointing exercise first.

Next bring your hand up and point at your face, exactly as you do in the pointing exercise. Get your attention looking in at your center and simultaneously aware of the pointing finger and the background beyond. Once you are relaxed in your center, you just start to rotate on the spot. The direction doesn't matter but I'd recommend moving quite slowly at first. Here's the sequence I recommend:

1. Start, by bringing yourself to center.

2. When you're suitably relaxed make sure you are standing up.

3. Stick out an arm and point your finger so that it is point directly to your face, so you can see the finger pointing straight at you.

4. Slowly start rotating on the spot. Keep your arm outstretched and observe. Now we have observable motion, but what moves? Consider only the present evidence. From zero distance, do you move or is it the room?

5. Speed up the rotation a little. Can you set yourself in motion? Can you move an inch at center? Staying focused on the stillness at your center, do you feel giddy?

6. Slow your rotation, slowing the room down until it comes to a gentle halt.

If someone is watching they will see you spinning on the spot while the room or place you are in remains stationary. In contrast, from your point at center there is stillness. You remained still while the space about you spun. When I do the exercise, I see the room beyond my finger moving past my finger but as I look inside I see there is no movement.

The spinning finger exercise reveals that at center you don't move. It reveals that you don't go to things, they come to you. At zero distance when you look at your finger you can see how you are perfect stillness. Reflecting on what you've observed, do you concede that regardless of what you've been led to believe you don't ever move an inch.

This raises into question the modern fear of speed? Why worry about all the hustle of life when you've never in truth budged an inch? The truth is you are always at rest, always were always will be!

MOVING SPACE

If you want further evidence that you are stationary, and the world is on the move, take a trip. Drive your car to the airport and from your center notice how on the motorway the lamp posts accelerate towards you and disappear either side of you in a blur. All the time things on the outside are speeding by, you are perfect stillness at center, totally untouched by the moving scene. You are always ready in each moment to accommodate the next object.

At the airport, you can board a plane, you sit and suddenly New York, or Paris, or Hong Kong is rushing to you.

To get to grips with your stillness I recommend you repeat the following exercise as often as you can.

WALKING STILLNESS EXERCISE

The exercise that follows is a very practical and easy to repeat version of the spinning finger exercise. To do this exercise you start by bringing your attention to your center while you walk somewhere. As you walk, simply observe your journey from center. Be still as the scene moves towards you, be silent for the sounds, be translucent for the colors and shades, be transparent for the solids to take shape be thirsty for the smells.

The great thing about the walking stillness exercise is that all you need to do to try this exercise out is to remember it when you are on the move and just give it a go. I don't know about you but I'm always on the move, so plenty of opportunities here!

This is the meditation that I do most days as I walk to work. What do you see as you walk? What I see, with awareness, is that I'm immobile, I'm going nowhere but most mornings the world and work comes to me. The office comes to Jamie. Jamie doesn't go to the office.

This observation enables me to experience my relationship with the world from a different perspective. At another level, it brings real peace into my movements. Where I used to mindlessly rush from train, to the underground and tube to tube before the final mad dash for the office. Now instead of all that rushing, I'm stillness and the office comes to me, or Starbucks comes to me, or New York comes to me and I never go anywhere, I never move an inch from my home.

There is a big bonus here for the traveler, what you will see is that the obstacle of space and time that have been keeping you from where you want to be, opens into the mystery. Every journey becomes an adventure. Every moment becomes an oasis of experiences. In an instant, you are cured of your sleep walking, lost hours are found, and frustration and boredom is transformed into inspiration and delight.

There are lots of variations of this exercise but driving the car is a particularly good application of the principle and I love doing it on the train. You might like to try it the next time you get on a plane, see if you go to Paris or Paris comes to you.

PEACE IN MOTION EXERCISE

It's my experience, that now I find peace, where before awareness, I found the most stress. It's a source of wonder, that now when I stand in a crowd, especially when all around me are rushing, I feel an ever-greater sense of my own peace. I used to be mesmerized by the rush of life around me, I used to join in it, excel at it. Now the buzz of life provides contrast that brings my own peace and stillness to the fore.

Next time you're in a busy place, bring yourself to center and take it in. See it all. Notice the contrast between all the things buzzing around the space. It's the space that is you.

Look for yourself, do you find the contrast between the frenetic activity of the world at large and your own inner landscape, do you find that this contrast brings to the fore a tremendous sense of peace and blissfulness.

SPEED

I'm sure that you've often felt that life moves too fast, most people do. Interestingly, despite what people are fond of telling you, this is not a modern phenomenon. It was a common complaint in ancient Rome, Antioch, Athens and even Buddha's India. If you don't believe me, reflect on what the ancients concerned themselves with! Take the time and listen to what they said.

It's ironic that as much as we like to complain about all the hustle and bustle of life, we seem to have an appetite for rushing around. As much if not more than people seek peace and tranquility, they also seek exhilaration and excitement.

I MOVE THEREFORE I AM

There is a logic that is driving this behavior, though it's quite twisted. When we speed up we seem to have a greater sense of our being a thing in the world. Remember the moving hand exercise from a few pages back. It's as if speeding up 'things' us. It makes us even more of a thing in the world, and of course our ego is desperate to be a thing in the world. Our ego is particularly keen to project that thing upon the world.

In contrast, when we idle, when we slow down, we can feel like we're nobody. It can feel like we are less than half alive. It's no surprise then that our irrational mind deduces it is well worth the cost in stress and strain, not to mention the risk, to be a thing in the world. To be a thing of substance not vagueness.

CLARITY ON THE LIMIT

An interesting thing happens as you accelerate. There comes a point where the sense of motion flips from you to the objects about you. It happens somewhere around 100 MPH when the sense that you are moving through the scene switches to a sense of stillness as the scene now rushes past us. When you reach speeds of over 150MPH it's all but impossible to ignore the sense of stillness in oneself as the scenery rushes past.

CALM IN THE STORM

It's ironic that we spend our whole life living under the impression that we are things flying around a static world. When, it turns out, that we are the calm at the center of the storm. We are the calm at the center of the mother of all storms! The truth is that the world and all things dance around us and their dance is chaotic beyond all measure.

You never move an inch and you never will.

BE READY TO SPEED THINGS UP

Don't be surprised that as you come to your sense you discover that your life starts to gather pace.

When it comes to the stresses of life the real solution is not to dumb things down, it's not to avoid life. The answer is not to take a pill so that you stop feeling the pain and anxiety. The answer is at your center, where there is enough capacity for 'All' and at center and as 'All' there is no stress. As your center, you are peaceful and blissful regardless of what is playing out within you.

As you become more centered, you will see the stress and strains that you used to feel abate. You will also find that you have much more energy.

All the energy you used to put into trying to change what is, or denying what is, or generally keeping up appearances is now released for good. You will find that you are living with more energy and that the contents of your stillness, suddenly becomes more energetic too.

This is a time when things happen, but in awareness you are ready, no longer resisting. In awareness, everything starts to flow through you. Life starts to flow through you unimpeded. You'll stop doing so much but so much more is done. You join the universal dance, but not as another dancer, you're no longer the little dancer to God's big dancer. No, you are danced and you feel the bliss of it all.

WEALTH AND ATTRACTION

OUR GUILTY SECRET IS IN THE OPEN

FOR MANY PEOPLE, money and wealth are dirty words. It's popular, especially in certain spiritual, religious and idealistic circles to denounce wealth and the wealthy. The truth is this tells you nothing about wealth but plenty about the denouncers.

The truth is there's nothing wrong with wealth, worldly success or money. However, there's often plenty wrong with what we think about them and what we think about ourselves and others in relation to them.

The same people that bemoan the wealthy will boast that they themselves don't want to be rich. But it's all rubbish! They are either being somewhat dishonest, to you and often to themselves or they are ill. It's normal and healthy to want to be rich, most people deep down feel they deserve to be rich. I think it's true that God not only wants you to be rich, he has made you rich. However, in your madness you can't see it and you can't enjoy your rewards.

This innate sense of a right to wealth should be taken more seriously, not denied or ignored. Hopefully, in this chapter I can help you to take this more seriously and start towards the wealth that is your due. However, this is a deep subject and one that we will return to.

STRESSFUL OWNERSHIP

For most of us wealth is tied up with ownership, we and society at large attach great significance and value to what we own.

For many the essence of great wealth is to have the thing you want, when you want it and to be free of it once you no longer want it. Part and parcel of this, is security, the sense that your stuff is safe, that things are yours and yours alone, and no one is about to take them from you.

You can start to see some of the stress that comes with wealth, and great wealth brings ever greater stresses. It's no wonder that so many of those with the greatest wealth, the greatest fame are the most unhappy and stressed people. Indeed, the wealthy are almost always far unhappier and stressed than the poor people around them that have so little.

One of the ironies of life is people cling to wealth, but it doesn't make them happy. They fear losing the very source of their stress and turn their back on a better plan that would let them have it all without any of the stress.

THE WAY WITHIN TO WEALTH AND RICHES

The 'Way Within' offers you stress free wealth, the unprecedented wealth which is your due. This is not a trick or some play on words, the wealth on offer is very real and having it is real too.

CASH IN HAND EXERCISE

For this exercise, you just need a coin, any coin will do. Start by relaxing as best you can, try to quite your mind down, then when you're ready place a coin in the palm of your open hand. Looking at the coin in your hand ask the question, does the hand own the coin?

From here looking at the coin laying in the palm is it not as sensible to say the coin owns the hand?

When I look I see that I have the hand and coin but there is no ownership between hand and coin. The relationship between hand and coin is simply of two things touching, each is occupying a bit of space and keeping the other out. There is some stress as they are brought together and resist each other insisting on their individual separateness.

Now, while still looking at your hand and the coin at the far end of your arm, notice what it is that is taking both hand and coin at this end of your arm.

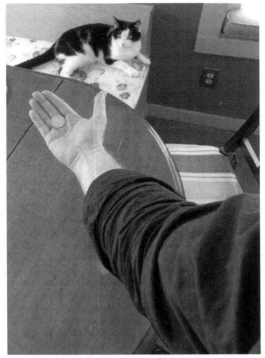

Figure 11 - Coin in hand with arm extending into the void

Take a moment to observe yourself as the capacity, the space, the no-thing that is open to arm, hand and coin. You are not resisting anything, see yourself as the no-thing that resists nothing. Become aware of the relationship between all. You as no-thing are not a fourth thing in this relationship, you are not adding another entity, you are not 'other' than these things.

Take your time but see yourself as arm, hand and coin right now. This is the ownership on offer.

THE TRUTH ABOUT OWNERSHIP

As things in the world we make such a big deal about what we own. We delude ourselves that we own this, and we own that. I own my house, I've paid off my car, and its mine. Others hoard share certificates in their safe that asserts their stake in this company or that company.

The truth is that things can never own things. In fact, things resist each other, they are mutually exclusive, insisting on themselves they are always merely themselves.

In contrast, as aware 'no-thingness' I ask for nothing, I'm open to all, all resistance is gone with no sense of separation. As 'no-thing' I take in all, I become all, I truly own everything I encounter.

You are only truly rich as 'no-thing', rich by your very nature not by effort, intent or acquisition.

THE END OF THE RAINBOW

Lots of people are looking for their treasure in the world, but it's a fruitless mission, it's a quest that is doomed to failure.

The treasure is only found through awareness, and it's found here and now. Nowhere else, no other time are you in possession of your kingdom come.

YOU OWN IT ALL

From your awareness observe the people that crowd the landscape in their poverty. They are shadows, bankrupt not owning the clothes they wear. As for the objects that you see, they are stripped bare, they are examples of perfect poverty.

Whereas, for you as the aware space, you need to see your essence as capacity and in that instant your riches are at hand; your kingdom is come, and your treasury filled. You are clothed and have the universe for your backdrop.

Everything that this moment furnishes you with is your property. It can't be any other way because this is how you are made, and you own the world in a way such that you can never disown it.

LIVING IN AWARENESS IS WEALTH MINDED

Much poverty, envy and disappointment comes from looking at other people and only seeing what you don't have. As aware capacity for all, this of course is never an issue. You just take it all in, no judgement. No desire other than to be the openness that you already are. In an instant, all that stress of keeping up with the Jones is blown away.

The stress is gone, but also in accounting terms your bank balance is much improved. The tangible improvement in your fortune comes as you stop buying things you don't really want or need, and as you stop buying things just to keep up appearances.

The irony is that the respect that you've been working so hard to garner by buying trinkets now flows to you from all quarters. Respect flows in, as people respect nothing more than someone that is true to their own purpose, someone that is authentic. The irony of irony that you'll find that the social ladders, the ladders that so many people are desperate to climb, keep extending for you exactly because it's all as nothing to your 'no-thing'.

People start helping you because they like you. They like and help you because they sense that you are not opposing them. If you totally embrace people and are wide open to them, although they can't quite fathom what's going on most people find your openness irresistible. Essentially, because you see, hear and are grateful for people just as they are, people are compelled to return the favor with interest!

Suddenly, you stop buying the trinkets, baubles that you thought made you something. Suddenly, you don't need a holiday, to look forwards to as a tonic for the stress and strain of your climb. Suddenly, you've stopped the holiday arms race and you don't have to go to exotic climates to cement your standing in society. Suddenly, you don't need a drink to sooth the pain at the end of the day or week.

You find that you enjoy a drink when you have one, and you love the place you are right now, whether that is Bali or Baltimore.

Again, the result is a swelling in your bank balance rather than your waist-line as you forsake the do-dads and lavish meals and concentrate on what you really want and need. What you really want, which is 'what-is' as opposed to 'what-is-not'!

NOTHING DEMANDS NOTHING AND GIVES ALL

Nothing doesn't demand anything of anyone. *Nothing* has everything, and everything is made up of *nothing*.

The lesson here is to be the no-thing you are, to stay true to nothing because what you will come to see is that no-thing always comes up with exactly what is needed in the moment, including the money that you now find you are less and less interested in.

ABSOLUTE WEALTH

This chapter is about your absolute wealth, but what we see is that as you become more aligned to absolute wealth and universal abundance your relative wealth tends to improve quite inexplicably.

Things and the relative wealth they bring can't be relied on, they can't be trusted. They represent a problem, they change, they perish they resist your ownership.

The aware no-thing, in contrast, doesn't change, doesn't die or perish. Only *nothing* can be relied on. *Nothing* delivers things, often not the things that you imagine you want, but it always comes up with the things you really, really want; the things you need. It shouldn't be a great surprise as it is from this mystery, this unknowable capacity that all things emerge for no reason. It's from this no-thing that the whole universe is emerging right now.

This is the power I'm asking you to put your trust in. The power to create galaxies and all they contain, all in perfect working order. If this power can't be relied on, what can?

ABUNDANT NONSENSE

There's much talk these days about abundance and scarcity as if we are talking about opposing world views. From awareness these become meaningless discussions, there is just what is and it's always the right amount at the right time.

Determining a situation to be abundant or scarce is judgement but from a different angle.

Despite all the chitter-chatter about abundance there's little wisdom to be gleaned from such thoughts. In fact, it's another trap, a trap that can only take you away from awareness.

There is not an abundance of things, there just is. There is nothing, then something, then nothing or so it appears. There is only ever awareness.

VALUE WHAT IS

Don't get me wrong, I'm not saying we should go mad and reap havoc and destruction because 'nothing' provides what we need. No, we should instead come to awareness and from there we are always in harmony with nature. We should cherish all the gifts the void offers, we should care love and care for all of creation.

It's probably no surprise that Accountancy is not borne from awareness, but a quick look at the accounting principles of everyday life and contrasting these with the accounting of the aware sage brings some valuable insights.

Most people in everyday life cut things up into the cost-able components and derive some overall value from the sum of the things. At work, we put a price on each step of our offerings e.g. we attribute costs to designing, building, delivering, providing service, getting paid, keeping the books and go about paying everyone their due including the business owners and government.

As a consumer, we do broadly the same thing with all our purchases. We consider what it costs to produce the product or service and balance that off against the benefits and decide if we are getting good value. I buy a nice bottle of Californian Zinfandel, it's on offer, and it's delicious. At £6.99 feels like a bargain. If I go deeper I could consider the effort of the vineyard to nurture these fine vines over many years, pick them at the right time, produce a good wine that needs to be stored, matured, bottled, transported half way around the world, then shelved. I might conclude that it takes £2 to get this bottle to me so I don't begrudge Waitrose, the grower, the importer, the various governments and a few others splitting the 4.99p profit. Lots of people must be paid for all this to happen and in contrast I only need to work a little to pay for it and it rounds of my evening to perfection. This sounds like good value.

Sadly, many of us don't draw this conclusion that we're getting good value when we look at the things we get and the money we must pay out, there's little gratitude in most people's worldly transaction, instead there is bitterness and bad feeling.

AWARE ACCOUNTING

In an everyday sense, this bean counting accounting works well. It clearly has its uses but from awareness it is the accounting of scarcity and bitterness. It is the accounting taken from the view of things, its second person accounting and I'm an aware first-person. As awareness, I no longer see what I get as the sum of a few parts. Looking at my shopping basket as a no-thing, instead of looking as my appearance as a thing in the world, I exchange all my worldly meanness for universal abundance and gratitude. Doesn't that sound like a better place to be?

To understand what I mean reconsider my bottle of wine. I pay the same £6.99 but in awareness I appreciate the true cost of delivering that delicious bouquet to my lips, the cost of bringing it all to me at exactly this place and this time to meet my need.

My calculation includes the shop assistant's salaries, the company's overheads, the cost of owning the land and developing the supermarket on it, plus the similar costs for the transport firms for bringing the bottle by road and sea, and the related middlemen and not forgetting the vineyard in California. Then there's the maintenance of the roads, ports, bridges, tunnels and as awareness I see that it cost the earth to get it here and now. From aware capacity, I can see that it cost more than the earth, it required the whole history of the universe to produce this one sip of wine just where and when I want it. It took all those ancient emperors that drew on ancient goblets and vine growers that tended ancient vines. As you take this in you know that the same is true of every service and everything that you take in.

I see how the cashier on till 18 who took my money and the assistant on aisle 4 who helped me find the Manuka honey were goddesses, they were none other than the universe itself in human form. This modest glass of wine is the end-product and reason for the entire universe to have existed.

This is a beautiful realization, gratitude is never again hard to find. Thank you!

THE UNIQUE CONSUMER

This is not just a lesson in gratitude or a reason for awe. If we consider a sip of wine with friends, you'll see that there's more to this than you might think. To help your learning, imagine yourself in a nice wine bar with friends and you are surrounded by groups of other like-minded consumers sharing conversation over bottles of wine and maybe some food.

From here you see various drinks vanishing into mouths set in the middle of faces. For you there's no knowing if it's wine or cranberry juice, coffee or frothy broth, hot or cold that is being drunk over there. Now compare this to what happens when you drink from your glass. Similar colored liquid is being poured into an abyss that is not framed by a face, or lips or anything at all. For you, red wine is instantly distinguishable from cranberry juice, coffee from soup, hot from cold.If you were to stay in this wine bar for years you would never come across another drinker like you. In fact, you turn out to be the only real customer, the only one who is served just what they ordered and the only one that is refreshed by the wine. You are the only one that leaves the wine bar without a face marked by stress and fatigue.

This accountancy that establishes that the whole set up exists for your benefit is the realistic accountancy. The other sort that sees you as just one of millions just like yourself is unrealistic. This is not to condemn the regular sort of accountancy though its essence is to deny your true nature. Your job is to enjoy, that glass of wine that was served up to the infinite, by the infinite and at infinite cost.

STRESS FREE OWNERSHIP

The essence of stress free ownership is to have what you want, when you need it and then to be free of it as soon as it's no longer needed. This is my definition of wealth. This is exactly what you have, as awareness. This state of being is unlike the experience of all the sad faced, stress riddled, millionaires. The same millionaires that most of us aspire to be.

I'm here again in my coffee shop enjoying a skinny latte. My accountancy makes me not just the owner of this coffee and the cup, but the whole shop; all of which has been provided by the unlimited exactly when I need it. From here, as I am, life is a pleasure. How very different my joy is from how it is for the legal owner of this little business, I saw him a few moments ago and he was a picture of stress and strain.

Who owns who? From here it looks like the owner is a slave to this place not the other way around.

From here I can see that the universe gives me exactly what I need, exactly when I need it but never makes a burden of things. As I walk into the night sky I'm rewarded with all the stars in the night sky, all for me, sparkling like a billion diamonds. As I look upon my treasure, my face is a picture of contentment. Where else would I put this treasure but up there safe and sound in the night sky. Would I have been happier with a certificate proving my ownership, a certificate which in any case would only ever be a record of me signing them over to me?

As your true self, you lose all the stresses of ownership which in any case is just a game of one thing claiming a few other things and in the process losing all. Instead of this, you can as 'no-thing' claim nothing and in so doing get it all.

As 'no-thing' you're never troubled by the fear of losing anything, you're never concerned that you're getting poor value or being swindled by a bunch of fat cats. Instead you take delight in a universe that's dedicated to serving you majestically with exactly what you need no matter what the cost.

Identifying with what you're not, identifying yourself as a body, an entrepreneur, a business owner, a success, a something in the world, a personality, is in the end cheating yourself. It's identifying with what you are not that is ruining yourself and it's a source of stress. Identify instead with what you are, with the 'no-thing' at your center, and you discover yourself to be rich beyond your wildest dreams.

THE LAW OF ATTRACTION

There is universal black hole out of which flows all that is created and into which all returns and is destroyed, everything is channeled from nothing and obeys the Law of Attraction. The law is the mechanism through which creation is manifest, it's not a cook book for would be amateur chefs.

The *Law of Attraction* is not a means for us to direct what is, it is a vehicle for what is to be manifest through us. You may think that the *Law of Attraction* can be used propel you along your desired path but if you misappropriate it you will inevitably head off down a deep dark dead end.

MIRACLES ON OFFER

It's popular to talk about miracles and manifestation together. My council, and the council of all the sages down the ages is to leave magic alone. Don't go looking for or expecting supernatural power to be bestowed on you to use as you see fit. Though of course the whole power of the unlimited is at hand.

The miracle here, is not that you will bend the will of God to deliver to you all that you think you want. No, the miracle here and at hand, quite literally, is that you will bend to the will of God, which irony of all ironies is all that you truly ever needed.

THE BLISS OF CO-CREATION

Creation comes from nothing and part of creation is about aligning with the universal purpose, your role is to align with this purpose. Once aligned there is only bliss.

This bliss is not only a kind of reward it's also your personal guidance system that directs and with awareness keeps you aligned with the universal purpose.

Follow the bliss!

RESISTANCE

Hand in hand with the bliss is resistance. Just like bliss resistance is a good indicator as to what is the right direction.

Resistance of what is or what might be is normally a good indicator that you are trying to hold on to what is not. You have fears and paradox is that you fear losing something that was never yours to lose.

When you feel resistance, don't flee. Instead, sit with it. Look where it comes from. See what it really points to. Stay with the feeling and observe. Let go and see what comes next.

THE ILLUSION OF THE MANIFEST

The *Law of Attraction* is a trap for many of us. It drags us deeper into material seeking. It's easy to be mesmerized by desires and the laws awesome power.

However, in the end what we manifest is always temporary. It's easy to get distracted by the illusion, it's easy to make things seem important. We can use the Law to change our circumstances. However, the changes are always ephemeral, and will evaporate in time. You can use the law to make a fortune, to become a something in the world. However, your true purpose here is not to acquire fame or fortune but to align with the universal will where you will find peace and happiness.

The *Law of Attraction* can't ever change what you are. It can bring things into your life, but no things can transform you. Things can't open your eyes. In fact, if you try to exploit the *Law of Attraction,* it's more likely you will end up closing your eyes even tighter shut and retreat into the dream of life.

You need to open your eyes and drop all the illusions.

BE CAREFUL WHAT YOU WISH FOR

I guess the point and lesson from this insight into the *Law of Attraction* is that we should be mindful of what we wish for. The point is not just that we should be careful but that we should be mindful.

I strongly recommend that you observe and note what you wish for. The simple and gentle act of observation is usually enough to undo the spell that will otherwise beguile you.

Until you have left your seeking behind you will always be manifesting from your ego. Until then, the things you long for are the things that will support the fiction of you, the fiction that you're trying to project onto the world.

For seekers, employing the *Law of Attraction* is never a fruitful way, it never leads then to lasting peace and happiness.

For now, we should be careful what we wish for, don't wish for things, power or change. You might well get the things that you crave but you won't get peace of mind, you will move further from where you need to be. Getting things, seeking power or making changes never transforms you. Such things never make you happy. At best, they just give you a buzz, a thrill or temporarily shake things up a bit. None of that lasts long.

The *Law of Attraction* brings forth what you want and that reflects who you are. For the unaware seeker, the law will only attract their ego, their fears and greed. You are not your ego, you are not your fears but that's what the law will make of your life, so beware, be aware!

HOW THE LAW WORKS

The Law brings forth what you resonate with and most seekers resonate with what they don't want. They outwardly seek wealth but what they are mostly thinking about, the feeling they have and therefore resonate with is a lack of money and that is the message that the universe gets and that is exactly what it will deliver.

The universe is just like my 5 years old, if I tell him not to drop something it's as if I said to him drop it and true to form accidents happen. In contrast if I say to him, carry the cup nice and upright that's what he does, no accidents.

The key to the law are the feelings you have. It's not the thought that is key, it's the feeling it leaves you with as this is what creates the vibration in you and it's this that the universe comes into alignment with.

GET OUT OF THE WAY OF LOVE

My council and my last words on the subject is love the law but don't meddle with it. Instead of dabbling with the Law of Attraction, live as a 'no-thing', and with no wishes other than for what 'is', let the Law flow through you and marvel at the wonders you and the universe can co-create!

Have that feeling of the wonderful and the law will bring ever more wonderful things to fruition.

Be prepared to be amazed, because from here on you will start to see what you love, and you will love what you see. It's hard not to love it when you realize that it's been gifted to you at infinite cost, and with infinite patience, and with perfect timing.

MORE IN-WAYS TO EXPLORE WHO I AM

AWARENESS EXPLORERS

IT'S VERY IMPORTANT that you try to do things from a place of awareness. When you have a moment just take in the space that is within you notice it's nature and explore its limits.

HANDS IN THE VOID

A good exercise for exploring the quality of your new found single eye is to do the 'Hands into the void' exercise. It's very simple, extend your arms in front of yourself and position yours hands about 14 inches or 35 cm apart as though you were about to clap with palm facing palm.

Now simply move your hands slowly towards your face while maintaining the gap between your palms, keep your hands moving until they disappear as they pass your ears.

You can bring them forwards and repeat several times. Pay especial attention to the edge of the single eye. Notice its lack of definition. You might want to explore it further by moving your hands around it as though there were a halo at the edge of your view.

This simple exercise is an excellent and accessible tool to explore the qualities of the single eye and hone your skills of seeing.

A good way to think about seeing is two-way looking, or what I've heard called apperception, which really means to see with awareness of the one that is seeing or put another way, to see with awareness of perception.

THE SINGLE EYE EXERCISE

Douglas and Richard are keen to talk about the single eye and this simple exercise is a powerful way of experiencing it for yourself.

Start by holding your hands in front of your face so that your thumbs and fore fingers come together in two circles like a pair of glasses.

Hold your hands in front of your face so you can peer through the two lenses that your fingers form.

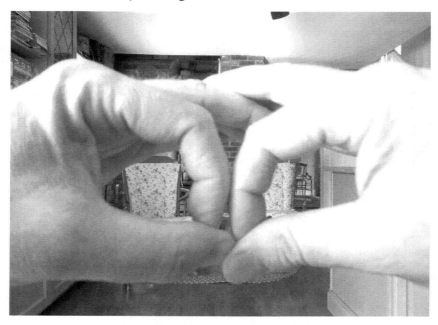

Figure 12 - Making glasses with my hands

You can see two holes where the lenses should be, two holes for two eyes to look through. Now slowly bring these hand glasses towards your face.

As they come closer notice what happens to the two holes. As I watch now the frame blurs until it dissolves into a single view.

Now this is how I've always seen the world, but for me I've rarely looked with this level of awareness.

Can you make out the edge of this eye? I can't look at the edge directly, but like the frames that dissolved, the edge of my view seems to gradually fade into nothingness.

Looking inwards as I look out I can't discern an end in any direction. I can see no end if I look up, not if I look down, not to either side, not in front and not behind. There is no end to the space I find at my center.

As I see it right now I can see my fingers dancing on my keyboard, and the train coach beyond. There are other people here but though they are in coach E of the 18:43 to Wolverhampton, none of these people share my view out. For all of us in coach E the scene constantly changes. For me, the site of the great train robbery flashes past to be replaced by Cheddington station. The man sat opposite of me is seeing scenes from Breaking Bad on his iPad. The people in this carriage see a turning page or maybe the face of the person that they are engaged in conversation with.

However, if any of my fellow travelers wanted to look in, their view and experience would be the same as mine and no matter how much the view outside changed the view in remains the same peaceful unchangeable, immutable 'I'. They would experience capacity and space for all. They would experience everything as part of them. They would know oneness. However, how each person interprets what is seen is unique to them. For some it is life changing, for some it is irrelevant and for others it remains totally unnoticed.

Now that you have a sense of the single eye, try to notice it as often as you can and over time develop an awareness of all its qualities as well is the contents it presents to you.

TWO-WAY POINTING

The 'Two-way looking' exercise is an extension of the basic pointing exercise. However, instead of just pointing in you simultaneously point both out and in at the same time.

It's easy enough, just start with your usual pointing hand in the position it reaches at the end of the pointing exercise; that is, pointing straight at your face. Then, when you feel centered. You point with your other hand, but this time with the index finger pointing away from your face, while the original finger still points in. I like to have my hands at 90 degrees from each other so that the knuckle of my inward pointing hand is against the side of my outward pointing hand. However, the exact configuration is not important what's important is that you are comfortable and that you can easily see a finger pointing in to your center and another pointing to what's in front of you.

Figure 13 - Two-way pointing hands

The exercise is great for exploring your new-found ability for bi-directional focus as you look in at yourself looking out at the world.

It's a perfect illustration of and gives you direct experience of apperception, where you are aware of yourself as awareness taking in the sights before you but unmolested by them.

USING YOUR BREATH

I find it very useful to incorporate my seeing exercises with breathing exercises. In general, I find it useful to begin each exercise by starting with a few moments of relaxation and conscious breathing where I focus my attention on my breathing where letting go of any tension I might be holding in my face, neck, shoulders, etc. go.

To help any readers that don't know what I mean, this is a typical sequence I might use.

I start by closing my eyes, but it's not necessary to have your eyes closed. I quite like to lie down but sitting is fine. I listen and observe any thoughts that are in my mind for a few moments. Just stay quiet and notice what I'm thinking about. For a few minutes, I'm just noticing my mental activity as its happing.

As I start to quiet my mind down I bring my attention to my breathing observing each breath. I follow my breath and notice any thoughts that come to mind. As any thoughts come to mind I just watch them. I find that if I don't engage them, don't take them up, they leave me be. As I breathe out I focus on the sensation as the tensions lift from me with each receding breath.

Watching is not an activity of mind. I don't think anything about what is arising. I just see my thoughts with a passive mind, with openness, with awareness. As an observer, I have awareness of thoughts. If I start to think something about my thoughts, I just notice the direction my mind is going, I notice this new thought about a thought. Sometimes if my mind starts to get distracted by thoughts I redirect my attention to my breadth and as my mind starts to calm down I wait patiently for the next thought and once again I'm back to observing the thoughts as they arise.

I repeat this observation of the breath until I feel my mind is nice and quiet. Then with each out breath I prompt myself to feel the tension going from a specific part of my body. I normally start with my face and I tell myself something like "As you breathe out feel the tension fall from your face, feel your jaw relaxing and your brow and eyes softening." I work down my body breath by breath.

When I come to parts of my body that are in contact with the floor or a chair I ask myself to feel my arms, back, legs, etc. sinking in to the floor. By the time that I reach my feet, I'm normally totally relaxed, and the background noise of my mind is all but gone.

I find that starting the exercises from this relaxed frame of mind makes it far easier to just take in what is being observed and I'm able to include any thoughts that may come to mind within this observation rather than being kidnapped by them. This creates an openness of consciousness that is appropriate when one is trying to come to terms with the openness of oneself.

SYCHRONIZING POINTING AND BREATHING

Something that I find useful, and I'll share with you, is an interesting extension of my personal conscious breath exercises into the two-way pointing exercise. This works particularly well with the two-way pointing exercise, but you can apply it to other exercises.

Put simply, as you breathe in follow your breath and look in, then as you breathe out look out from what you have just observed, look out from the spacious capacity at your center.

Perhaps it's a unique property of breath or perhaps it's something to do with the momentum that the initial breathing exercise creates but I feel that my vision inwards is clearer. I also find that I come to rest at my center more quickly and feel it easier to look out with awareness of the space I'm looking from rather than the objects I'm looking out at.

Explore all your senses. As you breathe out notice what you hear. Next breath notice what you taste. Next notice what you feel and notice how these sensations come together in awareness as you breathe in.

What do you notice? For me, because I've a kinesthetic bias, when my breath comes in I'm mostly aware of how it feels. For me each breath feels like bliss, then as I look increasingly out from center each sensation, each sight and sound is joyful.

The thing is to try it for yourself and then go with what works best for you.

WHAT'S HOLDING YOU BACK?

THE EGO GAME

EVEN AFTER WE'VE glimpsed the truth, most of us are held back and carry on with the old game of seeking and never finding. This game of seeking and never finding is a favorite of the ego because the game is perfectly designed for the ego's self-preservation.

KNOWING YOURSELF AT CENTER

Most of us are still struggling to make progress even after we've glimpsed ourselves at zero distance. We are easily distracted even though we've observed ourselves as spacious capacity. Even after we have sensed that we are open fully to the world, we find we are repeatedly drawn into the things of everyday life.

Looking out from your center you can encompass everything, looking in you are fathomless depth. At center, you are peace and you are free of your troubles. At zero distance, you see the world like a mirror sees its object, you see with perfect clarity, but you're not changed by the view. Just like a mirror, you capture what's before you and when it goes you are wiped clean. No trace of what went before lingers. However, what lingers in my experience is that old sense of being a mind in a body. The sense of being separate lingers.

In your everyday life, things are not played out from zero distance. In our daily routines and with the actions we take, things happen slightly removed from the center and they become stories we tell as 'me' and 'you'. With each event and each story something is added and 'me' is forever changed.

In contrast, at your center things pass without a blemish, not a word, image or thought is left behind with their passing. There is no desire, or need, or fear at center. Your center is the mirror of your soul.

Remember this, it is only ever 'me' that changes, the story changes, the illusion changes. The 'I' never changes, it remains forever perfect, not besmirched by sluttish time and never tarnished by grubby hands.

Keep coming back to this and each time that old sense of being a mind in a body arises, just acknowledge it for what it is, a lingering memory and let it go.

PICK OUT YOUR TRUE SELF

In your day to day life, you're probably far from the peace and fearlessness of your core. But, that peace is there, it was always there, and now you know it.

Until now, your true self was akin to radio static, always there but only coming to awareness when you mistuned your TV or radio.

Your center is like Andy Rourke's bass, he was always there when "The Smiths" played, always in the background, creating the space, driving things forward but when you bring your attention to the bass it explodes into your conscious attention, wonderful, beautiful and laced with genius! Just like listening to a single instrument in a song, when you focus on your center, your awareness is shifted.

Before this shift, the awareness that is who you are at your center, was always there, but you were unconscious of it. Now with awareness your center is unchanged, but now you know about it, you've experienced it. Sometimes your true self is in the background, sometimes it's in the foreground of your attention, but it's always present.

Now you know it's there bring your attention to it and it will burst forwards and fill your life with love, light and wisdom.

Right this minute because you're bringing attention to the awareness that is at your core, it's coming to the fore ground of your experience.

THE WIDTH OF A THOUGHT

Because you've known yourself as you are at zero distance, known yourself as capacity for life, this capacity is always available to you. Whether it's something you're aware of in this moment or even if it's something that's hovering quietly somewhere in the background, your true self is always available to you!

It always was there, and it always was available, but now you know your true self that knowledge changes everything.

In truth awareness is never more than the width of a thought away and all you should do is let the current thought drop away, let the thought go and just be aware space. You should stop being thought, literally stop being thought, stop being lived by and for your thoughts and let the thoughts just come and go. It's a call to wake up, stop thinking and start living!

LET LIFE FLOW

At the higher levels of awareness, you stop acting, and actions just happen. At this point you have moved out of the way and life flows through you unobstructed by your needs, fears and machinations. You are now always alert to possibility, but you are never tense, never strained you are always relaxed readiness and from readiness timely action flows.

IT'S TIME TO CHOOSE TRUTH

It's time for you to choose your true self and stop letting your thoughts keep you from your power and glory.

This is the only choice you have. Right now, you can wake up or you can go back to sleep. Your choice!

TROUBLE

If you take some time to think about your troubles. You will find that all your troubles happen when awareness is in the background.

Your mind drifts into the future or dwells in the past, fears bubble, past injuries ache, thoughts take over and judgement and suffering are where you're at. When awareness is front and center nothing can trouble you.

If things are troubling you, then you're not in awareness. That's fine because unawareness is where your work is!

The big difference now is that you have started to know yourself. Suddenly, you'll start to see when you're not in awareness. Whereas, in the past you just had troubles!

When you start to observe yourself, awareness will come to you and your troubles will be eased. You'll stop being your troubles, you'll watch them, just like you watch someone walking down the street, you'll leave them alone and they will walk right on past and out of sight.

This doesn't mean the things that troubled you before won't happen anymore. No, things will still happen, but they will just be things that need to be dealt with, things that are dealt with. They won't be a source of pain.

It also doesn't mean you're passive. You don't roll over and become a victim. No, no, no! You're not a victim because you've stopped all the thoughts from crowding in and you let the actions unfold from the center.

You do what you must do now! A miracle unfolds because reality starts to reflect the peace of your mind whereas before awareness, reality reflected all your troubles. Reality reflected all your crazy thoughts!

FEAR AND LOVE

There's only really love. Only ever love. Though in unawareness it can appear that there's fear and love. In general, it can feel like there's more fear than love.

By the way, if you are fearful you're not in awareness, you're in unawareness. Most of the time that you are in unawareness you'll find that there is plenty of fear and not so much love!

Again, being unaware is no big deal. Being fearful is not a big deal. The realization that you're asleep, the sense that you're sleep walking through your life in unawareness, and the notion that you're unaware in this moment or the next is a magic moment and in that instant of insight you cross over into awareness. You've opened the door to a life time of awareness. Fear and all those unaware feelings is a key to opening that door! The master key is experiencing yourself in a state of unawareness!

You've spent your life cultivating your fears. The little fears have bloomed in your mind and now they totally obscure your view. When you look now, when you look with awareness, you'll start to see that all fears are just thoughts. Erroneous thoughts at that!

There are many ways, gurus and even some doctors that will direct you to unwind your thoughts. They will encourage you to unravel your fear, remove the pain. That works, but it could take many lifetimes to clear the crud you've spent this life time filling your head with. There's also a bit of a problem as most of us end up adding new troubles, fears and pain faster than we clear them.

A ZERO-CENTRIC PATH

The Way Within is a zero-centric path. It's the direct path to peace and happiness. It's many lifetimes quicker than trying to unwind your mind, because like I just said, your mind will be winding itself up as you work to unwind it.

If you are zero-centric then you'll see that from your center, there's nothing obscuring your view. At center, all is clear. At center, all is colorless space waiting to be filled. At center, you are open to everything and anything.

Please take a moment to come home to your center and see what I mean. When you look, you appreciate that you are just spacious capacity for life and your openness is love. You are the space and the space knows itself. You are awareness that is aware of itself.

If at center you are clear and unchanged by what happens, if you are untroubled. This begs the question... if troubles and fears are not central to you, where are they?

Well, what you'll come to know as you look out from your center is that these beliefs and fears are still about, but they are off center. From here, at zero distance, I look sort of side on, squint if you prefer, to see them. If I bring these troubles here into awareness they dissolve in my light of being and truth.

You can see your beliefs and fears if you look carefully and when you see them you'll realize that they are not at center. Suddenly, you can see the 'me' that causes the fear. Your beliefs and fears are part of the fiction you created, the fiction you have spent a lifetime project-ing into the world. From center and in awareness you can see straight past the illusion instead of seeing with it. In awareness, I see past 'me' I don't see with 'me'.

WHO IS AFRAID?

This also raises another question. Who is it that is afraid? Or put another way, who is it that has all these troubles?

Come to your center and look for the 'one' that is afraid. What you find is love and total acceptance. Looking out you see your fears and troubles. They are never at center they are just thoughts that shape the story of who you are. The story of 'me'.

I'm not that. I am not 'me'. I am that I am. I am he that is. Not he that is not. I'm spacious capacity for life. I'm aware awareness and I am never afraid.

When I feel fearful, or when I perceive troubles which cloud my mind, I take a moment and look insides and try to find the one that has these troubles and fears. Here's the thing. When I look, I find no one that is afraid or troubles. Instantly, my fears and troubles are transformed if I just realize that he can't be found and that he doesn't exist. I still have problems, but now they don't trouble me. No, I should do what is needed and deal with life as it is; no fears added!

OBSTACLES

There are lots of sources of fear and the pain, and troubles that these fears bring are many. The key sources of fear are: other people's stuff, attachments, righteousness, non-surrender and desire.

So, the challenge for you is to be on the lookout for all these ob-stacles and each time you feel the fear rising or detect its symptoms like judgement, attack, and all the other forms of hate, you must look beyond the fear to its source. You must bring the fear and its source to your awareness where it will be revealed. Not only will the fear be revealed but all the darkness will be obliterated by the light of awareness.

You need to be a fear finder, don't be scared any more. Don't be down when fears arise, be delighted when you feel fear. Each fear points the way you must go, each fear is a step closer to your true peace. Bring them to the light of awareness, that's all, don't try to fix a thing, just bring your troubles home and they will release you from their grip. Just be with them, don't be in them and they will fade as you leave them be.

You bring fears into awareness by the simple act of observing them. Acknowledge them as being part of your story and you'll find that they rapidly dissolve. Mostly, you will have to repeat this several times, as thoughts and other triggers will continue to make the old fears rise inside you. However, in general these fears will feature less and less in your thoughts.

REVERSE YOUR ATTITUDE TO FEAR

I spent a lifetime running from my fears, seemingly avoiding them yet all the time spending too much time dwelling on them.

Paradoxically, avoiding fears ends up with you joining them. It ends with living them, they end up stored deep in your heart ready to rise again when a trigger event happens.

The 'Way Within' doesn't advocate going into your fears. The 'Way Within' encourages you to bring your fears into you. Don't hide from them, bring them into awareness. In awareness, just observe them, be with them yet at the same time leave them alone. In the light of awareness fears fade.

THE SEER

SEEING IS SIMPLE

SEER SOUNDS GRAND, but there's few things that are as modest or natural as being a seer. You need no gifts or special talents, seeing doesn't require great intellect or long years of hard study and it certainly doesn't require that you relinquish your old life and seek the peace of solitude on some mystic mountain top to attain the gifts of sight.

APPERCEPTION THE AWARENESS OF AWARENESS

If you have been doing the exercises, then being a seer is now well within your grasp.

You should be finding it easier to redirect the arrow of attention to focus it on the aware space at your center. Redirecting awareness from pointing exclusively at the object of your attention to the inner space in which the objects appear. Diverting attention from what's in front of you, or from what's in your past, or from what's in your future or from what's in other people's minds. The key is to bring awareness to attention.

I guess it's not strictly accurate to say re-directing your attention, as your attention can remain where it is. It's perhaps more accurate to say that you're expanding your awareness. You're extending your awareness so that it also takes in the place from which all things are observed, not just what is being observed. Awareness simultaneously of what is perceived and what is doing the perceiving is what I mean by apperception.

So, instead of just looking at an object you look in to see that there is an object in the spacious capacity that is your center.

So, you look both in at the center and from there out at the object of your attention. You move from perception to apperception. You move from ignorance to awareness. In perception, you experience what is seen. In apperception, you are aware that you perceive what is seen, you are aware of the process of perception, you start to see how you shape what 'is' into 'what is seen', and in the end this awareness liberates you from perception as all the things that get in the way fall away and you are left with what 'is'. It's what 'is' with absolutely nothing added. Once you stop adding to what 'is' then all you will bring to the party is your awe and wonder!

Put more simply, the seer sees not just what is observed but the observation also. The seer becomes aware of himself at zero distance. The seer is simultaneously aware of his private self at zero distance and his public self in the world at large.

The seer knows that there is no-body observing the world at zero distance, there's no little you at your center looking out or steering the ship. There's just the spacious capacity for everything, there's just the peace and openness that is your true identity.

There is just awareness. Awareness of awareness made up from awareness!

As a seer, you start to live your life aware of both the private self that is found at zero distance and the public self that you project into the world. The seer, doesn't need to take on any airs or graces, the seer doesn't need to assume a new persona or change in any way from how they were before awareness. The seer remains appropriate for others sake yet always aware.

WHAT IS AT CENTER?

You are spacious capacity, but what is this capacity made of? Is it made of the objects it contains? No! The spacious capacity is made of awareness. Awareness is the stuff of awareness. Awareness is aware space aware of itself. Awareness is all and all is awareness.

NO HIERARCHY AMONGST SEERS

You are seeing that you are not a mind in a body. You are seeing that body, mind, all objects and the world at large are all appearances of awareness. When you examine the spacious capacity at your center you find it is empty, a void in which all comes to be. You are not an object in the world, the world and all objects are in you. In fact, these things that are known, are perceived by a knowing self that is itself in awareness. They are known because you are aware-awareness. Awareness, awareness, awareness!

Here's the thing I love about seeing. If what is seen is nothing, and it is, then there can be no hierarchy amongst seers. No one can be better at seeing nothing than anyone else. No one can see more nothing than anyone else.

If you start to think that you can see more than someone else or if you meet people that claim they can see something that you can't then what they are talking about is something! They are imagining and that is not seeing, imaginings are a major barrier to seeing, though imaginings can be seen by the seer who knows nothing. In the end, the truth is we all see the same nothing. Though most people imagine they see something and nothing continues to elude them! Nothing is hidden because most people's attention is on something and ignores the nothing from which that is composed. Most people are not seers!

SEEING NOW

You're not present when you're dwelling on past events. You're not present when you're lost in dreams of the future. You're not present when you look at what's in front of you without awareness. You're certainly not present when you're stewing about what someone else might or might not be thinking. However, as soon as you expand your awareness so that you are aware of both the object of your attention and the attention itself, then you come into the present. With attention thoughts of the past, dreams of the future, other people's thoughts or the keyboard beneath your fingertips come crashing into the now.

Crashing is totally the wrong metaphor, because they just emerge and run their course but unlike in unawareness they are totally neutral, they come and go as they should without leaving a mark or ruffling any feathers.

Events will from time to time, stir up the old public self and you'll drop awareness. You'll head off down some rabbit hole shaped train of thought. However, with awareness, you'll see you're heading down a hole. You catch yourself and awareness returns you out of the hole. You'll see the public self from your private self and after a moments amusement these thoughts and feelings will just go on their way.

It's important not to get too hung up on the now. Getting hung up with the now is not of the now. At zero distance, all thoughts are in the now, you are in the now. The truth is that you are always in the now, how can you be anything else. It's just a matter of awareness.

SEEING WITHOUT EYES

When you come into awareness, when you settle at zero distance you'll notice that you're no longer looking out with the body's two eyes. You are just the aware space. You're this boundless capacity that is always open and everything is taken into you.

You've stopped moving, the world now moves, and it moves within you. Nothing to see out there, it's all in here. You are the world seeing itself.

NON-DUALITY

It's most common to experience the world as a duality where you are the subject that observes separate objects. From this perspective objects are separate from you. God is separate from you. The universe is separate from you. As a seer this distinction, this separateness is removed. At zero distance, there are no distinctions between objects. At zero distance, there is no separation between objects and subject, no distance. Everything exists in you. Everything is created by you. Every experience is played out in awareness, everything is made of awareness. There is a kind of collapsing in until you see that awareness is not in you, you are in awareness, there is just one awareness and all things arise within it and are made of it and merge back into it.

THE QUALITIES OF SEEING

Douglas Harding sets out the key features of seeing in "On Having No Head" as:

- Most accessible and obvious
- Fool proof
- Deep
- Same for all
- Always on tap

SEEING IS THE MOST ACCESSIBLE AND OBVIOUS THING

It's hard to be specific and clear about where my search started or indeed what it was I was looking for, but quite early in my quest I came to believe that the path to enlightenment was not for the faint hearted and it required years of dedication and sacrifice.

In the early days of my journey I was in awe of those that had gone before me and wondered if I would be able to follow their footsteps, did I have the discipline and persistence and courage to overcome my fears?

Fortunately, there are many ways that will get you home. There are also as many paths as there are souls to be guided home. I don't wish to detract from any other way, but I have come to realize that the 'Way Within', this Headless way, offers us a route that doesn't have to be as hard as we've been told. In fact, it doesn't have to be hard at all.

The Way Within reveals that the truth isn't hidden. However, a bit like when someone cunning hides something precious by placing it in plain sight, the truth is much harder to find because it's staring us in the face.

When I started my search, I was looking for something other than what I was, I was looking for something else. Along the way, I came to believe, that I had to change. I came to believe that I was somehow wrong and needed correction. My skills were wrong, my attitude was wrong, my beliefs were wrong, my thinking was wrong, my clothes were wrong, I was wrong, wrong, wrong!

However, what I finally found is what I Am. What I Am, is what I've always been and always will be! I wasn't looking for that. Not many of us are looking for what we already are. So, it's no surprise we manage to overlook what is right where we already are. This is how we all miss what is so beguilingly hidden in plain sight!

Well, it turns out that seeing is the most obvious thing in the world which is in direct contrast to what most of us have been led to believe. We have been looking for what we imagine, not what 'is'.

It turns out that Nature is always in plain sight and it's available now, and it's available to us all, just as we are. It doesn't require that we are gifted, saintly or special in anyway. It's like Wittgenstein said, "The aspects of things that are most important for us are hidden because of their simplicity and familiarity."

It turns out that seeing is the most accessible and obvious thing. This is in direct contrast to what we've been told which is that it is inaccessible and mysterious.

SEEING IS FOOL PROOF

This 'No-Way Way', this 'Way Within' is fool proof if you take the time to look. If you follow the exercises, and take what you see on face value, you will experience awareness knowing itself as awareness.

You can't get seeing wrong, you can't be somewhat sighted, or half sighted. Take a moment now and see if you can get seeing wrong.

It doesn't take intelligence or knowledge. As I keep telling you, intelligence and knowledge can be something of an obstacle. It does, however, take a little practice. Mainly because it's hard not to judge what you experience, and it's hard not to overlook awareness altogether because you come with other grander expectations. This tendency to judge and presuppose is a habit you must let go of. Letting go of judgements and presuppositions will come with a little persistence and awareness.

SEEING IS DEEP

Looking down into yourself, looking at your center, you start to appreciate that you have capacity for all. When I look down I can see no bottom. As I explore the space within I can find no edge, no end in any direction. The capacity extends forwards, up, down, sideways, behind, going on forever in all directions and for all time.

When we look in we sense that even the greatest distances that we can observe are near compared to the depth of this space we are at center. The distance to the far-flung galaxies is as nothing when compared to the available space within.

SEEING IS THE SAME FOR ALL

Our public self, which of course is a fiction, is as unique to us as is our body. But our private self is universal. Interestingly, our public self, the persona people meet and can touch is not just unique to our self, it's unique to every person we meet. No matter how much effort I invest in creating the fiction that is me in the world, how I'm seen is different for every single person on this planet. It turns out that every single person on the planet interprets what I'm projecting based on their personal beliefs, experiences, mood, conditioning, time, temperature and a million more variables! One person imagines me selfish and another selfless, all at the same time and all reflected in the same act.

Now anyone can see 'me' on the outside but only I can look inside and see the 'I' that is to be found at my core. Likewise, only you can look to your 'I'. However, what we both find is not the uniqueness that we'd always imagined ourselves to be. Nor do we find another 'me' inside me, we don't find another 'me' behind the 'me.' When we look for the one that has the feelings, fears or sensations of being 'me' we find no one.

At my center, I find only spacious capacity, a no-body and no-one. This is what we find, and this is that we are. We are without beliefs, ideas, judgement yet blessed with blissful peace and free from all fears.

Through this simple enquiry, we find that we are a private self and a public self. The irony is that the private self that we think is so unique, is common to all. Whereas, our public self is unique to every person that sees it.

This insight into the private and public self can change everything for you. Take a few moments to think about what it means for each personal interaction you have. For me, I can see how I've always at some level treated everyone that I've met as competition, as different from me, as separate from me and as a threat to my uniqueness and goals.

Now, with awareness I can see people's public face and I'm totally open to that. In awareness, I let it all in, I let you all in and I recognize that behind the façade we are the same 'I' that is at the center of me.

Something else that you might want to dwell on is that the experience you have of your private self, is the exact same experience that a Buddha, Jesus or Master Eckhart had when they looked inwards. What Douglas Harding pointed out as 'Headlessness' is where we find common ground; there's nothing at our center to disagree about and there's nothing idiosyncratic.

Unlike our subjective reality this experience can be communicated without any distortion. For example, I might think that Jack Black is hilarious you might think him a bore, I might think a dress is pink you think it cerise. Whereas if you look within you can experience the truth of your nature exactly as I do. We can both experience our true nature exactly as all the mystics down the ages have done.

When I was a young man I worried endlessly about what people thought of me. Then as I got older I protested to anyone that would listen that I didn't care what people thought about me. Finally, in my more mature years and with awareness I've come to realize that no one was ever thinking about me. They were all far too busy thinking about themselves and struggling to keep up their own fiction. Most people are too caught up in themselves to give anyone else any real thought or attention.

As a seer, I've come to realize when most people looked, they only saw themselves. They saw their prejudice, their beliefs, and their story of me which of course was only ever their story of them. They saw it all and still never saw me.

Take solace when people hate, cheat or bore you because it is only ever themselves that they hate, cheat and bore. You are untouchable! It's ironic though, laughable that it was only ever me that hated, bored and cheated me, the irony being that I am never 'me' or that.

SEEING IS ALWAYS ON TAP

One of the great things about coming home to yourself at center is that once you've found yourself you will know the way home and be able to return in an instant. At first, you can repeat whatever exercises work best for you but with a little practice and the knowledge that you have gained from practicing, your inner peace and your true nature is never more than the width of a thought away. With practice returning to center becomes as easy as redirecting your gaze from the sea to the sky.

This is good news because the place you need is at hand when you need it most, no matter what your mood, no matter your state of mind, peace is never more than a thought away.

More great news is on because you can anchor this place so that you can instantly return with a click of your fingers.

THE ONENESS PARADOX (NOT ONE, NOT TWO)

We are as one, yet we each have a unique perspective on the world. The paradox is profound, not one yet not two.

This paradox is not an exclusively human phenomenon, it extends to the whole universe and beyond and it includes God. Not one, not two. Don't over-think it, let it go for now and forgive me for talking about oneness when in practice I'm talking not one, not two.

I'm not looking at what you see right now, and I don't bring your history, genes, beliefs, etc. to the party. However, if I look inwards all this is here in me, as it is in you, and when I let go it is all on tap for me, as it will be for you when you let go too.

ALL OR NOTHING?

You might find that you get caught between being all things and being no-thing. I think most of us get a little lost around this point. This is confusing, am I nothing or all things?

In the end, it's equally true to say that you are all things and nothing. However, it's simpler to just say "I am."

ANCHORING AT CENTER

If you want, you can anchor yourself to your center. Simply follow whichever technique you prefer for reaching yourself at center and then create an anchor. You'll need to select a new anchor, maybe the thumb and forefinger of your left hand, then just repeat the process for anchoring your attention to your center.

If you need a refresher on anchoring the instructions are: first, simply bring your attention to yourself at center, then press together say your thumb and forefinger of your left hand releasing them before your attention wanders from center. Repeat several times ideally repeating often over a several days.

HAVING SEEING FRIENDS

LONELINESS

I THINK FOR many of us, and certainly for me personally, seeking was a lonely time. Coming into awareness takes the loneliness away. At least to the extent that you are no longer lonely. You may continue to have lonely thoughts, it's just that they are less frequent and don't trouble you like they would have done before awareness.

After awareness, you might have the thought, I'm lonely. However, now you see it's just a thought. It's just a thought, it's never what you are. I am not lonely. I am not that. I might have feelings of depression, but I am not that, I am not depressed.

Before awareness I might have said to the world, or more likely to myself, "I am lonely" or "I am depressed".

When I say something like "I am useless", I attach myself to that thought, I define myself by a thought; in a sense, I become the thought. After awareness, the same thought of loneliness, depression or uselessness might come but there's no association, no attachment and it leaves me unchanged!

LONELINESS IS AN ILLUSION

After awareness and after you have dropped the notion of being a separate mind / body, loneliness is just one more illusion that drops away. Like many bodily feelings, it will linger. However, the lingering will not be sustained if you embrace what has been seen. If you drop the notion of separateness, then how can you be alone? That would require that there is something outside awareness that you are separated from.

Embrace awareness and identify with awareness as the 'I am' that is aware; then you see that all things are modulations of awareness. There can be no sense of lack. When you know awareness, there are no objects, no subject, no time and no separation. Just awareness and it is known by awareness.

When loneliness does arise, just observe it, breathe and notice where it comes from notice how the feeling changes your physical form, leave it alone don't play with it just watch, notice and let it ebb away.

AWARE FRIENDS

For me, there is something extra delicious about the nature of awareness and that is the joy of sharing the wonder of it all. Being with another soul that has seen the truth, being with another soul that no longer needs belief to prop them up, being with another soul that doesn't need anything. Being with someone that is simply taking in what 'is' and wallowing in all the abundant joy and having fun. Being with someone like that is a joy for anyone, but for the awakened it is a special treat. It's the magic of the one recognizing the one, love loving love in the light of awareness. It's taking a cosmic shower with someone else.

Seeing is not the end, though it's probably the beginning of the end of your seeking. There's much work to be done and it's both a pleasure and a relief to have others that are either striking out into this new country or have already walked some of its ways. Having seeing friends can make the journey easier and lighter. Having seeing friends is a wonderful thing.

FRIENDS TO SHARE THE BURDEN OF AWARENESS

The truth can seem like a bit of a burden simply because it's what most people need but are lacking. The problem for you, the burden you will have to carry, is that most people are not quite ready, willing or able to fully embrace the truth.

As you come into awareness the lack of awareness in others is apparent. This obvious need people have for the truth is matched by a desire in the newly awakened to share the truth. However, all things are not equal because what people need is not generally what they want. Although paradoxically at another level it's what they really want, it's what they've always wanted.

As the desire in you emerges to help others, to tell them the truth that you see so clearly. Observe it, acknowledge it and let this desire to help others go.

Bear in mind also that what for you is, right now, the most fascinating of insights, is for others either odd or boring. This is another reason that it's something of a relief to be with people that you can share your experiences of awareness with. It's a relief to be with people for whom you will be neither: a bore, a crank or an annoyance.

Socrates and many others through history have suffered from the need to share the truth, a truth that people needed but didn't want. Socrates was called the gadfly and inevitably it was always just a matter of time before his society swatted him.

I'm not saying don't tell the truth. Not at all. Always speak the truth. Always be authentic. I'm saying at times keep your own council and don't be a bore. Don't try to teach pigs to sing, they have awful voices and will hate you for your efforts.

THE TRAP OF HELPING

Helping is another trap. The trap arises from the illusion that you know what anyone else needs. This knowing thought that is born from unawareness. It is born of judgement and naivety. Only the ego thinks it knows, awareness knows that it doesn't. Awareness trusts what is, it is what is, and awareness lets go.

THE HEADLESS CIRCLE

Another benefit of seeing friends, or those friends that are at least happy to explore the Way Within, is that willing friends open many opportunities. Opportunities for new ways to experience truth. Quite a few of the exercises Douglas and his friends devised require more than one person. A favorite of mine is the headless circle.

The procedure is very simple. You need at least 3 people but a few more is better and 10 is ideal. Stand in a circle and put your arms around each other's shoulders so that you are close and there are no gaps. Look down so that you see just a circle of bodies.

As you stand in the circle looking down, you get a sense that you are separate. Notice how your body disappears somewhere above the chest and that all the other people in the circle similarly disappear.

Figure 14 - Headless circle from above

As you bring your awareness to this single eye view, notice how all the heads have disappeared into this single eye. There are not lots of eyes, just the one and everyone in the circle is inside it.

Figure 15 - View from inside the headless circle

From inside the circle and looking down you see torsos, legs, feet and floor all disappearing upwards into the void above.

Private thoughts are not shared in the circle. However, the one-ness that is at everyone's center is revealed. It's the no-body that is at the top of the circle. The exact same no-thing for all. Once again, when you see who you are from zero distance you also see who every-one else really is too.

One important insight from this experience of oneness, is that you don't ignore the differences that you see down there. The seer has room for all points of view. What appears separate down there is joined in oneness up above.

Richard Lang describes the circle as being like a round temple that has lost its roof, the temple having no roof is wide open to the clear boundless sky. You are this sky, the sky of being. You are the one that is many. From the circle, you see that you are not one, not two either; you are oneness. You are awareness.

WHERE DO YOU GO FROM HERE?

THE PARADOX OF LETTING GO

I'VE SAID IT many times, seeing is not the end, it's another beginning. Seeing is the bridge between the world of the sleeper (the world of illusion) and the world of awareness and truth. Seeing is the way out of a life of seeking, but when you leave your seeking behind what are you left with?

It's paradoxical, that our spiritual path is one of letting things go rather than picking new things up. The paradox is partly that though you let things go, you lose nothing. When you see clearly, what is seen is just how much more you must let go of.

THE FINAL CHOICE IS YOURS

Armed with the insights we have been sharing, the choice is yours, you either choose to live your life from center or you go back to your slumbers.

With the 'Way Within' you choose to embrace the practice of being at center and extend it to every aspect of your life. You choose to be zero-centric rather than ego-centric. You choose to use this zero-centricity as the basis of a spiritual life, a mystical life of love, peace, understanding and purpose.

When you live at zero distance you can bring all your troubles to the light of awareness and see them drop away. In the light troubles and fears drop like the old skin that they are. The truth is that in awareness it's easy to let go of things, whereas before awareness it is all but impossible.

It's not all plain sailing. There are still many side paths and traps waiting for you. It's easy to form new attachments and these can create real blind spots. New attachments will block your line of sight, obscure the truth and give you their version of things. Amongst the worst attachments are spiritual attachments.

Don't get too big for your boots, stay humble and keep going back to center. It can be hard to be humble when you're gripped by the awesome. So, don't be surprised if you get caught by this trap, and don't be too hard on yourself if you do stumble.

Make a habit of observing yourself. Keep a keen eye out for sudden emotional responses, anger, fear, jealousy, nervousness or any other negative state of mind. When these negative states of mind bubble up, be calm, watch them like you're watching someone else, watch them with indifference. Look behind these negative thoughts and feelings for the source, the attachment. This observation of your stream of consciousness brings what you find back to the light of awareness. You don't have to do anything more, just let negative thoughts be and they'll go on their way in their own time.

Don't force things, don't try to change your mind or modify your thoughts. Be warned, any attempts at thought correction or even replacement with positive thoughts drags you away from awareness. Leave them and they will leave you!

SEEING AS A BEGINNING NOT AN END

Seeing is not an end, but it should be the end of your slumbers. You have a life time to explore. You're an adventurer in virgin territory and what is revealed is what was always there, but you'll know it as if for the first time. You're free on every level and now you can use the rest of your life to live with what always was and always will be or you can live an illusion. The choice is yours.

Master Umon tells us that the first step on the Zen path is seeing into the void nature and Douglas Harding adds that getting rid of our bad karma comes after, not before, that seeing. We've just taken the first step. We've opened the void before you and now you must jump in!

So far, you've had a glimpse of the truth, it takes practice to make seeing your normal way of being. It takes some commitment from you to get to that point where you can always see from beyond other. It takes practice to achieve the perfection of seeing as oneself:

> *"We stop seeing others and start seeing only one-self."*
>
> *Chauang-Tzu*

I love this quote as it so gets to the issue of seeing:

> *"The foolish reject what they see, not what they think; the wise reject what they think, not what they see."*
>
> *Huang-Po*

Observe things as they are and don't pay attention to other people. This is the choice you have; to be wise or to be foolish.

So, next we must make a practice of living with what we have seen and not be lived by our thoughts. It would be crazy to be lived by thoughts of what is not there, wouldn't it?

Are you alive to your thoughts or are your thoughts alive and manifesting through your body?

For me the challenge or perhaps the key to peace and happiness is to start loving what 'is' instead of seeking what 'is not.'

The next challenge for you is to move from having glimpsed the 'no-thing' that is your essential nature and the common ground from which oneness springs, to a consciousness of really knowing nothing yet with an acceptance of everything. Or more succinctly:

> *"To one who knows nothing, it is clearly revealed."*
>
> *Meister Eckhart*

There are two aspects to this. First, there's the fact that you can know nothing other than yourself, which is liberation and freedom.

Second, there's the getting to know yourself at center from zero distance.

These two aspects of your experience come together in a beautiful symmetry:

> *"There's no longer any need to believe when one sees the truth."*
>
> *Sufi Al Alawi*

From zero distance, you can see that everything has facticity but no meaning. By this I mean things just are, they are totally neutral. What we think of a thing, place, situation or indeed anything reflects our current thoughts. The meaning is what we add to the facts and it is this added meaning that we experience not the reality. This is the illusion.

AWARENESS THERAPY

If you are struggling to let go of troubling thoughts, clearly someone telling you to let go of negative thoughts is not always helpful. If you're in pain, saying, leave thoughts or even watch them but with indifference is a tough pill to swallow. Often, it's just one more thought, it's just more fuel for the fire.

If you find it a struggle to let go of your negative thoughts, just start by focusing on the space the thoughts are in. Nurture awareness of the space that your thoughts operate from. Now looking out from your thoughts to the surrounding field of awareness what do you see? How is the space affected by the thought? What else is coming into awareness?

The redirection of attention from painful thought to awareness of spacious awareness often creates the space for the thought to relax its grip on you. Then you can observe the thought, you can start to let it be, and maintain a new level of dispassion towards the thought.

IT'S NOT ALL LIGHT

The initial euphoria of seeing at zero distance and moving from your slumbers to wakefulness is often followed by the Dark Night of the Soul.

Obviously, we can't know how this is for others, but seen from a far it's not so bad. What it 'is' is different for each of us.

In one sense, I guess the sense of darkness is really a question of contrast. If you've got lots of dark truths to face and you drop them all at once the change is going to be blindingly profound and the light will be deeply unsettling.

THE LONG DARK NIGHT OF THE SOUL

For many, the length and darkness of this time is emphasized by the traps they have fallen into at the very moment of truth. The most common trap is to start to identify yourself with your journey. To become attached to what you've become along the way. It's harder to get a sage, seer or holy person to ascend through the gates of heaven than it is to get a child to skip through.

This dark time is mostly about dealing with the last vestige of ego. For many, the last hiding place and the best place of concealment for the ego is your halo and holy robes, your mantra, your sacred objects, meditation and especially God.

Not at first, but bit by bit the ego will pull you in, and moment by moment the gloom will descend. The contrast between the light of revelation and the darkness of ego is depressing.

In this matter, the light of awareness can work wonders. Observe from your center and the specter will be revealed. The light of awareness will purge all the darkness from your soul.

Few that have gone before had the advantage that this vantage point offers. How lucky are we, for to be forewarned is to be forearmed! This knowing of what to expect means that it is easier to see through the dark ahead and even enjoy this unfolding.

For many, the way out of darkness was long and lonely. The most common path is to rid oneself of the holy self is through un-holiness.

THE UNHOLY PATH TO WHOLENESS

It's not enlightened to sit up on high resting on your ideals and lord it over all. It's better to have tasted all of life and be able to take or leave it rather than to judge that things are not for you even though you've never actually known them in awareness.

It's a bit like the stages of man. As a child, you learn that wealth and worldly pleasure are not good, for the holy man, the holier than thou man, strives to live a good life, a pure life but perversely they never really drop the sins.

For the holy, and when I use the word holy I really mean the holier than thou crowd. For the holy, sin is what defines them. Holy people set themselves to live in opposition to sin. The irony is that sin is therefore their guiding light.

Holy people are always uneasy, always tense and resisting. They're not authentic. They're not truly holy. Being holy is just what they're doing, it's not what they are. Holy is what they are trying to be, though they can never be other than what they truly are; all roles are an illusion.

In contrast to the holy, or at least in contrast to the holier than thou, you know the saint for what he is, the saint never knows his saintliness. The saint never does anything saintly. For the saint things are done!

From the point of view of awareness, every action is holy. Everything happens in the holy moment and everything is perfect. Then, there is the error, the moment of illusion, when we add something. We add something that is not there, something that is never needed. We add a judgement, good or bad and the moment is lost. We never add anything to the present moment we add it a moment later.

DROPPING THE UNHOLY

It's easiest to drop 'sins' if you have tasted them for yourself. It's easiest if you embrace them fully, if you open to them. You must walk a long way from your holy house, you must eat well of all of life if you are to come back in awareness and drop it all. This is the story of the prodigal son.

Now in awareness you can be child-like but never a child. You will no longer be holier than thou, but you will choose to do whatever must be done in the moment. You will choose it because it's right not because of some moral or law, and never as an act of defiance or resistance.

THE DUSKY TEA TIME OF THE SOUL

Awakening is different for all of us. For some it can be less the long dark night of the soul and more the dusky tea time. For some the problem arises when they start to do nothing. Nothing can happen; but you mustn't make it your practice. The 'Way Within' is not a path to nihilism.

It's easy to become an observer of your soap opera life only to find the actor playing you forgets to show up and read his lines. If this happens, then from here on in it's like watching a car crash in slow motion. You're watching it from the back seat and start thinking I wonder what it will be like when the car hits, when you should be in the front seat doing what is needed in the now to steer the car to safety.

This nihilism and despondency is not awareness, its voyeurism and it's an easy trap to fall into.

The way out is the way in. The way out is to be in the moment, to be open to what is needed of you and do it with purpose. Observe the thoughts that arise, however, focus your energy on action don't get distracted by the thoughts that will continue to bubble. Notice these thoughts, acknowledge them but be action, don't succumb to doubt or fear or judgement. Don't be blind though. Be ready for the moment when the current action needs to be changed, don't add more to the insight, you just need to change. No need to feel bad or to worry or to regret not changing sooner, just do it.

DON'T SUCCUMB TO NIHLISM

You should observe these thoughts of self-destruction and apathy. Bring them into the light of awareness and realize that you have been only half awake, you've been day dreaming. You've been fantasizing, and you should be aware that all thought creates something. So, be careful what you choose to think. You've been adding something to what 'is' when nothing was required other than to stand as awareness.

Standing as awareness makes you the instrument though which creation flows. Whereas, you've left God flying solo as the creator, when your role is to work with the universe as co-creator.

OVERCOMING DOUBT

You might also find that you're faced by much self-doubt and questioning. In practice, you will probably be faced with many questions and an uneasy sense that it isn't worth it. Whatever 'it' is.

However, if you expect all this, if you expect doubt, if you expect it to get darker before dawn, it can make dealing with it all so much easier. There's nothing wrong there just 'is'.

I like to use the alarm metaphor. Look at it this way, you've been comfortable in your slumbers and the alarm's just gone off. It's 6AM and you've got to get out of bed to face an uncertain world, a world where you need to make your own way. In awareness, you get up each morning and offer the universe your hands, your eyes, your heart, your voice so that life can flow through you.

It's no surprise that all this is somewhat disconcerting, and people hanker after their bed. You could say you're faced with the choice, face the world, find your way without any support or go back to bed where it's safe, soft, warm and familiar. The world is full of sleep walkers.

It's not surprising that so many of us even after we find awareness press the snooze button a few times before we finally haul ourselves out of bed.

THERE'S NOT REALLY ANY GOING BACK TO SLEEP

There's an important thing that you should consider before you turn over and go back to sleep. You can't find the light if you are looking for it in the dark.

I think it's impossible in the long run to totally return to your slumbers. Once you know that everything you need is here, right now and it needs nothing adding, it's hard if not impossible to fall back into a deep sleep.

PRACTICE

It's perfectly natural to feel discomfort as you awaken. This is all new, being at center and plunging into the light of awareness will feel uncomfortable and awkward at first. You need to keep practicing until a capacity for two-way seeing into and from the void becomes your norm. Persevere with this seeing until it requires no effort. Practice, practice, practice and spend as much time as possible exploring your zero-centricity.

THE RESURGENCE OF YOUR TRUE NATURE

Your true nature has a habit of growing of its own accord. Trying to force it can have disastrous consequences. In effect, if you consciously try to shape your true nature, or speed its development along, it becomes a new you, a new 'me' and that means the ego is back in charge again, and you've got even more to let go of!

Your true nature needs no guidance, nothing needs to change. You just need to see through all the nonsense and illusion that obscures it. The noise that drowns it out. The thrills that numb you to what 'is'.

THE LONG AND THE SHORT WAY

One thing that is unique about the journey is that this is a journey of no distance. The place you are seeking is the width of a thought away and thoughts occupy no space.

Therefore, with the 'Way Within' you can bypass the long winding road that is common to many other ways. It's paradoxical that with the 'Way Within' you must drop all the things that get in the way of *seeing*, *being* and *loving*. The paradox is that you can skip straight to awareness of your true nature without having to let go of a thing.

The 'Way Within' not only allows this fast track, it's part of the way. Remember what Douglas said about seeing first, then dropping all the bad karma. Having seen your true nature as awareness it is much easier to drop all the illusions. Seeing makes dropping all a necessity and seeing gives you the ultimate tool, the light of awareness.

LIVING WITH THOUGHTS, NOT AS THEM!

SEEING, BEING AND LOVING

YOU SHOULD KNOW by now that there are many paths but the essence of them is always the same. The ingredients are always the same but how they come together and in what proportions, is unique for each of us. How you experience this process depends on where you are now, what you've learnt and your innate qualities and talents.

In simple terms, the elements of the path are *seeing, being* and *loving*. The purpose of your journey is to embrace these aspects of yourself. The nature of your journey is letting go of whatever is stopping you from seeing, being and loving. Your journey is about dropping all the illusions and knowing yourself as you are. The thread that connects them all is thinking. Paradoxically, you'll have to drop your thoughts to be free to see, be and love.

We have dealt with seeing and as such you should at least have awareness of the difference between seeing what 'is' as opposed to looking through what you are and seeing what is not.

With luck and a good tail wind you will have had some first-hand experience of seeing. By this I mean seeing yourself as open capacity for life. With luck, you'll be well on your way to making this facility the cornerstone of your life's journey.

Don't be overwhelmed by all this. Remember what I said earlier, seeing comes before dropping bad karma. Dropping illusions doesn't have to be completed before you can come home. Much easier I think to come home and then drop the illusions.

For all of us, thinking and our thoughts are the real source of our suffering. You must learn to live with your thoughts, not through them and begin to make peace your normal state of mind.

Once we have put thinking to bed we will come to the final element, love! Now, love will have featured in everything that you've done so far, but we need to let love come to the fore. This is a simple extension of seeing what is and is made easier for those in possession of a quiet mind. Love is the catalyst for the final surrender. Everything changes when love stops being an activity or experience and becomes your complete outlook. When love is your outlook you will pass through the eye of the needle and finally find heaven on earth.

THE JOURNEY FROM SEER TO SAGE

As a Seer, you have observed what 'is' with nothing added. As a seer, you have observed reality without what you think should be added and without ideas being added.

As a seer, you have seen yourself as 'me' a self-created fiction and you have gone on to see past yourself. You have seen as the 'I' that we all truly are. You have come to rest in the 'I' and seen it as spacious capacity open to all, but not affected by anything. You have experienced the peace within. You have seen that your mind and body are just objects in awareness. You are not a mind in a body, you are the awareness that is capacity for all. More than this you are the knowing of awareness.

You are unlike modern scientists, they see the world as a third party, they observe as a third person singular where everything they observe is changed by the simple act of observation.

You have seen the world as the subject, as 'I', not as an object in the world. You have seen the world as a first-person singular where everything in the universe is within you. Everything is within you. There's not a single thing that alters what you are at center. At center, you are the abyss from which all of creation springs, a mirror that reflects all yet is never changed by anything.

In the changelessness, you have glimpsed your eternal-self. You have tasted the immortality that is at the center of who you truly are.

The next part of your journey is to learn to live with your thoughts not be lived by them. This mastery of thought, coupled to the ability to see, is the essence of the state of being I call being a sage. This bring us back to my earlier quote:

> *"The foolish reject what they see, not what they think. The wise reject what they think, not what they see; observe things as they are and don't pay attention to other people."*

> *Hang-Po*

I almost don't like to add to this, and it seems somewhat ironic, but I'm tempted to be a little more expansive and say, "Observe things as they are, don't add to them, don't ponder other people or dwell on yourself."

As a sage, you must go beyond the sense that you are the subject (awareness) that contains objects. As a sage, you must drop all sense of separation. The sage sees how there is no distinction between subject and object. No distance no separation.

When we talk about the space of awareness it is a metaphor. Don't get attached to it. Awareness is not like space. It's not like a room where objects are brought from outside to furnish it. There is no outside. All things are in awareness, all things are conjured from and dissolve back into awareness.

Dealing with the journey from seer to sage is not a small topic and it requires more attention than I can bring in this single volume. The aim here and now is to get you to see, get you to drop the old view of yourself so that you can be ready for this journey from seer to sage.

PRACTICE

PRACTICE AND WISDOM

WORDS ARE BEAUTIFUL, for some they are easy to come by. However, it's what you do that counts, not words. Wisdom has little to do with what you know, and even less to do with what you say. Wisdom is exclusively a product of what you do.

For most of us it takes quite a bit of practice to do most things, and that is also the case with seeing. So, rather than leaving you to head straight off and read another book, as was my normal practice, I'm going to suggest a routine for you to take up and if followed it should help to anchor seeing as your normal state of being.

I'm also going to suggest that you don't read anything else for at least 28 days.

TWO TYPES OF PRACTICE

You can either make practice a chore or a way of life. To understand what I mean practice is either a matter of a regular routine, where you are completing exercises with purpose and discipline. Alternatively, practice is about using the techniques and mindfulness in everyday life as and when it is needed.

This second sort of practice is about bringing awareness to everyday life. It's about employing awareness whenever there is a real need to act mindfully, responding mindfully to events. Practice when there is a need to deal with your thoughts and feelings about events rather than practicing as a chore when there is time at hand but no immediate issue.

Regarding what we've learnt of the 'Way Within' it may seem that daily participation in the exercises is somewhat unreal. Daily completion of exercises in the comfort of your home or wherever you choose seems contrived. Whereas, it may occur to you that using these techniques when faced with fear or any of the associated negative emotions is more meaningful and constitutes a high level of wisdom. However, the snag with being mindful when really needed, is that you must remember to be at center and open. More specifically you must bring yourself to center and be open to 'all' at moments when you are most contracted and most apt to forget.

Routine practice, in relation to the 'Way Within' has the effect of increasing the peacefulness and openness in all aspects of your life. Practice kindles awareness until it's a raging fire that illuminates all corners of the world. It makes sense then to practice when we are least stressed so that we are prepared for the times of great need.

There is a word of caution; you need to be careful not to get too attached to the practice. For this reason, I encourage you to mix it up in terms of when, what and where you practice. Avoid getting institutionalized into only practicing the same exercise at the same time in the same place. Otherwise, you might end up like the meditator that though sublimely peaceful at home on his mat, goes nuts when someone treads on his toe on the subway and has no peace until he is back on his mat and regurgitating his mantras.

In the end, life provides the perfect playground for you to explore the practices we are talking about. Just be alert. When you feel contracted then let go of the thoughts that are closing in on you, and instead open to what 'is'. Each time you forget to be open and centered, don't treat it as a failure, and don't beat yourself up. Smile, because if nothing else you can now imagine yourself being aware, you know of a better way, and you are willing to be better. Surely, that little stumble is one less slip you will take before you finally find your feet! Remember babies don't go from their cots to running marathons. There's lots of rolling, crawling, toddling, walking and running to be mastered first. You wouldn't berate a two-year-old for not being able to ride a bike just because you've shown them one and told them what to do. So, why be so hard on yourself when you don't instantly make the transition from your slumbers to full awareness.

A FRAMEWORK FOR PRACTICE

I'm going to suggest a routine. However, please feel free to mix it up. There's a worksheet that you can find on the resources page of my web site www.waywithin.com you can cut and paste as you see fit.

I think it's a good idea to come up with your own schedule that resonates with you. Don't be lazy, make sure you include those bits that you found difficult or just plain didn't get, as these are perhaps the areas of your greatest need.

Feel free to add any other exercises that you've picked up.

SUGGESTED ROUTINE

In outline the routine is as follows:

1. Start each day by reading the notes in the worksheet that relate to today's exercise.

2. Look for opportunities throughout the day to practice the exercise of the day or put its lesson into practice. Look out for times when you feel contracted. Be alert for when your dominant thoughts are negative as this is a signal to apply the exercise of the day. However, if when you feel contracted or negative a different exercise comes to mind, then don't be rigid, go with it, give this alternative exercise a try. Failing all else, just work on your breath, just breathe.

3. After a week, start the new week by doing the next exercise in sequence. I've listed 8 exercises. So, on the first day of week 2 do exercise 8, on the second day do exercise 1. This way you don't do the same exercise each week on the same day.

	Monday	Tuesday	Wednesday	Thursday	Friday	Saturday	Sund
Week 1	1	2	3	4	5	6	7
Week 2	8	1	2	3	4	5	6
Week 3	7	8	1	2	3	4	5

Figure 16 - Table to illustrate exercises by day and week

EXERCISE TIP

Something I find useful is to record myself saying the exercise of the day on my phone. I simply read out the exercise, then when it's time and I'm sitting nice and relaxed I just listen to the recording on my phone and follow the instructions.

Check out my web sites resources page I may have the scripts and some recording loaded by the time you read this:

http://www.waywithin.com

DAY 1 – ANCHOR IN THE NOW

You're going to produce an anchor by bringing your thumb and forefinger together while experiencing the sensation of awareness in each of your senses. Through repetition the sensation of awareness is associated to the anchor so that you can later return to awareness by simply repeating the movement of thumb and forefinger.

First anchor your body (the Kinesthetic sense)

To do this, start put your book down and then do the following:

1. Relax and close your eyes. Send your attention into your body. Try not to verbalize your feelings, just become aware of raw sensations.

2. Once as much of your attention as possible is focused in your body squeeze the index finger and thumb of your right hand together to make a loop. This is your 'anchor', hold the anchor for a few moments or until you feel your concentration on your body wane or your concentration in general starts to drift away, then let your finger relax. Ideally, you'll relax your finger before your attention drifts.

3. Repeat this exercise several times. Each time use the thumb and forefinger of the right hand. The anchor will be made stronger by repetition.

Next repeat the anchoring steps but this time focus on your sense of smell and taste (Gustatory sense):

Anchoring the Gustatory Sense

Pick something that has some taste and smell. You probably need to repeat for both smell and taste. I like to use gum for taste as I'm not tempted to swallow it and it keeps its flavor.

1. Relax and close your eyes. Send your attention into your taste buds and nose. Try not to verbalize your feelings, just become aware of the flavors or aroma.

2. Once as much of your attention as possible is focused on the taste or smell you are experiencing squeeze the index finger and thumb of your right hand together to make a loop. Hold the anchor for a few moments or until you feel your focus or concentration start to drift away, then let your finger relax. Ideally, you'll relax your finger before your attention drifts.

3. Repeat this exercise for some different tastes and smells several times and in no particular order. Each time use the thumb and forefinger of the right hand.

Anchoring your sense of hearing (Auditory Sense)

Next repeat these steps for your sense of hearing:

1. Relax and close your eyes. Send your attention into what can be heard. Try not to verbalize your feelings, just become aware of the sounds, picking out the foreground then exploring the background. Bring your attention on to each sound, maybe a bird song or police siren or some people talking in the distance.

2. Once as much of your attention as possible is focused on the sounds you can hear squeeze the index finger

and thumb of your right hand together to make a loop. Hold the anchor for a few moments or until you feel your concentration drift in anyway, then let your finger relax. Ideally, you'll relax your finger before your attention drifts.

3. Repeat this exercise several times for a range of sounds. Each time use the thumb and forefinger of the right hand to anchor your attention.

Anchoring your sense of sight (Visual Sense)

Finally, repeat these steps for your sense of sight:

1. Relax and close your eyes. When you feel relaxed slowly open your eyes and take note of what you can see. Send your attention into what's being seen. Try not to verbalize your feelings, just become aware of what you can see.

2. Once as much of your attention as possible is focused on what you are seeing squeeze the index finger and thumb of your right hand together to make a loop. Hold the anchor for a few moments or until you feel your concentration start to drift away, then let your finger relax.

3. Repeat this exercise several times by looking at whatever you choose. There are no right or wrong things to look at. The important thing is to associate the act of looking with the anchor so that you can bring attention to what is being seen.

DAY 2 – POINTING EXERCISE

The procedure for pointing is as follows. With your preferred hand point at a distant object or feature.

Figure 17 - Pointing at a distant object

Take a moment to note what you see, for example the objects color, texture and its position relative yourself. Consider the other senses. Consider any sounds and how it feels to you. Is it part of you or separate?

Keeping your finger pointing directly at the object and wait for a few moments. Reflect on whatever is being pointed at before moving your finger.

Move your finger so that you're now pointing at the ground in front of you. Again, take a moment to take in what you're pointing at. Consider its color, distance, texture, density, feeling and your relationship with it.

Now point at your foot, either foot it doesn't matter which. While pointing at your foot focus your attention to the foot in question and take note of what you see, maybe a shoe or sock, note the texture, color and how this foot feels different from the floor you were considering a couple of moments before. Are you separate from your foot, are you inside the foot is the foot inside of you?

After a few moments reflection move your finger so it's pointing at your knee. Likewise, let your attention flow to your knee. Again, take note of your knees shape, color, texture, and its distance from you. Reflect for a moment on these things and how it feels. Is it an object, is it separate from you, are you inside that knee or is it inside of you?

Next rotate your finger so that your hand is pointing directly at your torso. Again, follow with your attention to where your finger is pointing. Take in the texture, color and sensations that you find when you follow where your finger leads.

Finally, and most importantly rotate your finger again so that now it's pointing directly at your face. I find about 6 inches is a good distance. Now look where your finger is pointing. Literally direct your attention away from the pointing finger to the place it's pointing at. Take your time and look at the place, be aware of the place you are looking out from. It's not the hand that you can see there, instead of the hand you are focusing on the place you are seeing from. The place that sees the hand. The place that is aware of the hand.

Figure 18 - Pointing at my center

What can you see? Keep your attention on where the finger is pointing at and ask yourself:

Do you see any color or structures there?

Do you see your face or any signs of a head?

Do you see your finger, arm, torso and those little legs?

Are you aware of the space at your center?

Do you have the capacity in you for all?

Is it this capacity that you look out from?

Does this capacity take everything in?

Is the space itself transparent?

Are you in this space, are you made from space or are you this space?

At center we're spacious capacity, take a moment to observe this space, sense its openness, and know your true nature as clarity and openness.

As space we don't judge, we just accept everything. As space, we're perfectly at peace with everything that comes our way, accepting all, loving all. As space, we're free of all the ideas, beliefs and opinions that have ruled our life for so long. They are not part of who we are at zero distance. At zero distance, we're aware space with capacity for all.

As we look out we can't see a head. Where we've always thought that our head was, there is just this big space. No eyes are seen but one single view is revealed. My face is not here for me, it's there for you!

At center, I don't want anything to be other than it is, I'm totally open to what is.

DAY 3 – PEACE IN MOTION EXERCISE

Today's exercise is one of the simplest. The exercise exploits the contrast between the bustle of a crowd and your own inner peace to help you to experience your true nature.

The exercise just requires that you place your self in a busy place. Anywhere will do, a supermarket, rail station, outside your place of work when everyone is arriving in the morning. The location doesn't matter.

Once you're in a busy place, bring yourself to center and take the scene in. See it all. Notice the contrast between all the things buzzing around the space before you and the space within you; the space that is you.

Look for yourself. Do you notice any contrast between the frenetic activity of the world at large and your own inner landscape? Do you find that this contrast brings to the fore a tremendous sense of peace and blissfulness?

It's my experience, that as I stand amid life's hustle and bustle I find peace. Whereas, before I knew awareness, I found only stress in a crowd. It's my experience that we can only find the peace that we have been seeking by being right here, right now. Thinking back, I used to run away from the here and now naively expecting to find peace elsewhere. I was looking for peace somewhere else sometime else.

It's a source of wonder for me, because now when I stand in a crowd, especially when all the people around me are rushing, I feel an ever-greater sense of my own peace. I used to be mesmerized by the rush of life around me, I used to join the rush, excel at it. Now the buzz of life provides contrast that brings my own peace and stillness to the fore.

Now when I move with speed, it's a choice made in awareness and it's a joy. These days I love the sense of motion because I enjoy the busyness of life without the old anxiety and insanity.

DAY 4 – HANDS IN THE VOID

A good exercise for reacquainting you with your single eye is the 'Hands into the void' exercise.

It's very simple, extend your arms in front of yourself and position your hands about 14 inches or 35 cm apart as though you were about to clap with palm facing palm.

Now simply move your hands slowly towards your face while maintaining the gap between your palms, keep your hands moving until they disappear as they pass your ears.

You can bring them forwards and repeat several times. Pay special attention to the edge of the single eye. Notice its lack of definition. You might want to explore it further by moving your hands around it as though there were a halo at the edge of your view.

This simple exercise is an excellent and accessible tool to explore the qualities of the single eye and hone your skills of seeing the space within, knowing it and seeing from it.

DAY 5 – TWO-WAY POINTING

The 'Two-way looking' exercise is an extension of the basic pointing exercise. However, instead of just pointing in you simultaneously point both out and in at the same time.

It's easy enough, just start with your usual pointing hand in the position it reaches at the end of the pointing exercise. That is with the pointing finger pointing directly in at the space within.

Then, when you feel centered; you point with your other hand, but this time with the index finger pointing away from your face, while the original finger still points in.

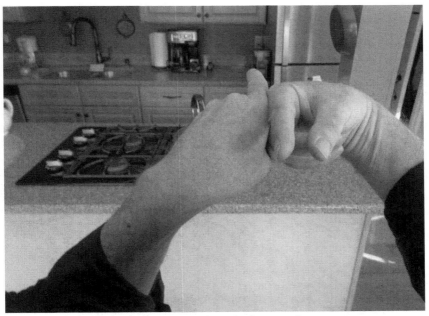

Figure 19 - Two-way pointing - looking out from center

You'll probably find the exercise experience enhanced if you combine it with conscious breathing. Put simply, as you breathe in follow your breath and look in, then as you breathe out look out from what you have just observed, look out from the spacious capacity at your center.

As you breathe in be aware of your breath, pay attention to it as it fills your inner aware space. Attend the breath, feel how your lungs are experienced in awareness. Know the experience of lungs filling. As the breath flows out notice how this is a movement only in awareness. The breath flows from awareness of the inner to awareness of the world. You never know your lungs filling with air, you only know the experience in awareness of lungs filling with air. You never know breathing out, you only ever know the experience of breathing out. All that is ever known is the experience in awareness. You are the knower of awareness.

The exercise is great for exploring yourself as spacious capacity for life. Your capacious nature is revealed as you look in at yourself looking out at the world.

DAY 6 – THE SINGLE EYE EXERCISE

This is another simple exercise to experience yourself as the single eye of awareness.

Start by holding your hands in front of your face so that your thumbs and fore fingers come together in two circles like a pair of glasses.

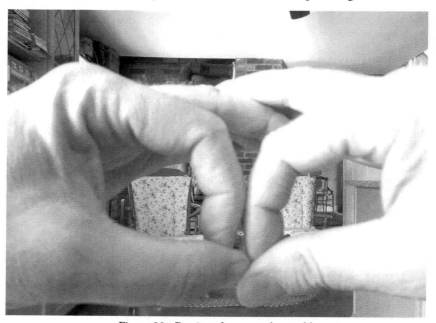

Figure 20 - Putting glasses on the world

Hold your hands in front of your face so you can peer through the two lenses that your fingers form. You can see two holes where the lenses should be, two holes for two eyes to look through. Now slowly bring these hand glasses towards your face. As they come closer notice what happens to the two holes. As I watch now the frame blurs until it dissolves into a single view. This single view is how I've always seen the world, but for me I've rarely perceived with this level of awareness.

Can you make out the edge of this eye? I can't look at the edge directly, but like the frames that dissolved, the edge of my view seems to imperceptibly fade into nothingness.

Looking inwards as I look out I can't discern an end in any direction, not up, not down, not to either side, not in front or behind.

How does it appear to you right now?

If you choose to look in, your view and your experience is the same as my experience and no matter how much the view outside changes the view in remains the same peaceful, unchangeable and immutable 'I'. The thing that is different, and it is different for each of us, is the meaning we extend to this vista.

Join me now and experience capacity and space for all. Come and ponder what the experience means to you. To help you in your pondering consider the following questions:

> As you do the exercise do you experience everything as part of yourself?
>
> Do you start to sense oneness?
>
> Do you still feel attached to the sensation of being a separate body?
>
> Does this perspective mean anything to you?

On this last point, don't sweat it. It's fine if it doesn't mean anything, examine your feelings and try to avoid imagining something special. Instead, just observe and pay attention to what feelings you have and what meaning you take from these exercises. Try to avoid adding meaning what you see.

Now that you have a sense of the single eye, try to notice your single eye as often as you can and be aware of all its qualities as well is the contents it presents to you.

DAY 7 – WALKING STILLNESS EXERCISE

To do this exercise you simply bring your attention to your center while you walk somewhere. As you walk, observe your journey from center. Be still as the scene moves towards you, be silent for the sounds, be translucent for the colors and shades, be transparent for the solids to take shape be hungry for the flavors.

What do you see as you walk?

What I see, with awareness, is that I am immobile, I am going nowhere. Now in the morning the world and work comes to me. The office comes to Jamie; Jamie doesn't go to the office.

On one level, this observation helps me to experience my relationship with the world from a different perspective. At another level, it brings real peace into my movements where I used to mindlessly rush from train, to the underground and tube to tube before the final mad dash for the office. Now instead of all that rushing, I'm stillness and the office comes to me, or Starbucks comes to me, or New York comes to me and I never go anywhere, I never move an inch from my home.

There is a big bonus here for the traveler, what you will see is that the obstacle of space and time are the very things that have been keeping you from where you want to be. The walking exercise effectively 'opens up' space and time into the mystery.

Every journey becomes an adventure, every moment becomes an oasis of experiences. In an instant, you are cured of your sleep walking, lost hours are found, and frustration and boredom is transformed into inspiration and delight. In the end, you find that you are always here, in the very place you have always sought.

There are lots of variations of this exercise but driving the car is a particularly good application of the principle and I love doing it on the train. You might like to try it the next time you get on a plane, see if you go to Paris or Paris comes to you.

The big lesson here is that you don't have to be still for the motion, stillness is what you are. You don't have to try to be silent for the sounds because silence is what you are. You don't have to try to be translucent for the colors and shades because translucent is what you are. You don't have to make space, you don't have to be open to accommodate everything because you are openness and you accept all and finally you start to see how you are all.

DAY 8 – THE SPINNING FINGER EXERCISE

Spinning the world needs nothing just your time and it needs a willingness to give it a go. Spinning the world needs willingness to examine what your see. This exercise is a great way to get a sense that the world moves through you rather than that you move through the world.

The procedure couldn't be simpler. You start by bringing yourself to center. If you have anchored your center use your anchor. If you can manage to center yourself by simply directing your attention to your spacious capacity, that's wonderful, do it now. If you can't just center yourself try doing the pointing exercise first.

Next, once centered, bring your hand up and point at your face, exactly as you do in the pointing exercise. Once you are relaxed in your center, you just start to rotate on the spot. The direction doesn't matter but I'd recommend moving quite slowly at first.

Now we have observable motion, but what moves? Consider only the present evidence.

From zero distance, do you move or is it the room?

Speed up the rotation a little. Can you set yourself in motion? Can you move an inch at center? Staying focused on the stillness at your center, do you feel giddy?

Slow the room down until you come to a gentle halt.

If someone is watching they will see you spinning on the spot while the room or place you are in remains stationary.

In contrast, from your point at center there is stillness, you remain still while the space about you spins.

When I do the exercise, I can see the room beyond my finger moving past my finger but as I look inside I observe that there is no movement.

The spinning finger reveals that at center you don't move. It reveals that you don't go to things, they come to you.

At zero distance when you look at your finger you can see that you are perfect stillness.

Reflecting on what you've observed, do you concede that regardless of what you've been led to believe, you don't ever move an inch.

This raises into question the modern fear of speed? Why worry about all the hustle of life when you've never in truth budged an inch? The truth is you are always at rest, always were, always will be!

ADDITIONAL EXERCISES

You might want to mix it up a bit more by introducing one of these exercises:

> THE HEADLESS CIRCLE (Page 220)
>
> 'FACE' TO 'NO FACE' – THE TUBE EXERCISE (Page 161)
>
> MOVING HAND EXERCISE (Page 168)
>
> CASH IN HAND EXERCISE (Page 180)

The tube exercise requires a willing friend and the headless circle requires a group of friends. Similarly, you might want to drop some exercises from your rotation.

THE END IS YOUR BEGINNING

WORDS OF ENCOURAGEMENT

THE 'WAY WITHIN' is not about adding a single thing to what you are. No, the path you will follow leads to the letting go of a lot of stuff and this does take time.

The other thing about letting go of things is that it works like a big fly wheel. At the start you work hard, and in time and with persistence the wheel starts to move. At first, it's hard to see any movement, but steadily the flywheel gains momentum until, bit by bit, it has enough energy to keep itself spinning.

So, don't be discouraged if you don't immediately transform into a being of light. Be gentle on yourself, after all you've been subjected to decades of social pressure and you have absorbed a life time of beliefs. It takes time to let all this go.

Seeing itself is easy to grasp, yet most if not all of us find it hard to keep this seeing business up. This is where practice helps. Keep doing the exercises and increasingly you will see as capacity for all rather than seeing as just another object. You will live as a first-person no longer 'thing-ing' yourself into second or third 'persondom'.

YOU CAN'T GO WRONG

Don't be discouraged if you don't get the benefits of seeing straight away. To be frank you'd be truly exceptional if you did. Transformation will be yours, but the timing of things is a question of grace and not favor. You must do the work, you must see, be and love; and then it will come when you are ready. Paradoxically, it won't come when you think you are ready as that's a whole lot to much thinking and desire for things to be other than they are. Let go of wanting 'it' and just love what 'is'.

Don't for a minute think that you are not doing things right; you are doing it all perfectly. When we look inside, we see it all. We might not appreciate it all because our mind gets in the way as thoughts crowd our awareness out. However, rest assured when it comes to re-directing our attention towards the aware space, the space that is our true nature, you can't 'more or less' see yourself as spacious capacity.

You can't get it wrong. However, it might not mean a whole lot to you right now,

You might not immediately be aware of the impact of this new point of view, but the effects on you are, from the very first glimpse, are profound and certain. You won't realize but behind the scenes, the subconscious giant is at work and it is busy establishing itself. The genie is out of the bottle now and it's out forever. You won't discern the transformation as it slowly builds, you'll start to see more and more from zero-distance, but you won't notice it happening, until one day you'll be open to all and it will just seem natural, nothing different.

It's most likely, that you'll be the last person to notice all these changes, we tend to immediately recognize stress but not its absence as a no-thing. Besides, because your awareness is more and more at center, and at center you've always been perfect, so there are no changes there to notice!

Because it's already perfect, the improvements are not visible for you to see at center, but they are clear to those on the outside. These changes are for them and not for you.

What is for you is the bliss you'll find as you are, as you've always been, with nothing added and nothing needed.

FEELINGS

Feelings are something of a two-edged sword. Earlier in the book I talked about how they can be used to guide us along our path. However, their usefulness arises from their extremes. You know when you are on the path because you feel the bliss and you know when you have strayed because you feel fear, pain and a myriad of other negative things. There's no getting away from the fact that negative feelings can be very disheartening and discouraging.

It's natural to question the effect and effectiveness of the 'Way Within' when negative thoughts crowd around you. You have seen yourself as capacity, and you intellectually get it but inevitably you will feel rotten if you are plagued by doubt and fears.

Don't be disheartened when old fears return, or new fears grow. Welcome them, acknowledge them, then steer your course and leave them behind.

Maybe an onion is a better metaphor than the fly wheel I used before. If we think of the way as peeling an onion, and our path as all those layers that must come off.

When peeling onions our eyes tear from the start and that doesn't stop as we take off the layers. So, it is with letting go, you've got so much to let go off and so many tears to shed, but in the end, we will be left with nothing and there will be no more tears. By nothing, I mean you will be left as you are, the ultimate no-thing from whence all comes and to which all returns.

You might be confused as I said that the 'Way Within' is a direct path. This is true, it's a direct path to self-realization; you get to know yourself. The transformation though occurs at the level of knowing. Whereas, our beliefs and the associated fear and pain is all stored at a cellular level. Consequently, it takes time after awakening before you are free of your legacy beliefs, it takes time for the associated fear and pain to fall away. The real spiritual work happens after you become aware.

The good news is that it is lighter work when done in the light of awareness, it's far lighter work when compared to all those seekers that are trying to do the same work of undoing in the shade of an indirect path.

In effect it is after enlightenment, after we know our true nature, that the true work begins which is just the allowing of all the stored beliefs to arise so that we can finally be free of them. We free ourselves by finally letting them arise, acknowledging them without engaging in them and then just letting them go on their own accord.

Don't be too worried about this now. Don't let a single fearful thought discourage your practice. Be guided by these fears, let them serve you rather than serving them. Don't feed them with your life force, take from them instead. They point to the resistance within you, the resistance which is always fighting what 'is'. Let this resistance go, let creation flow!

Don't add doubt to your existing woes, you don't need something else to let go of.

The thing for now is to see and know yourself as you are, to know yourself as spacious capacity for all. I will dedicate the next volume of the 'Way Within' to finishing off this onion! If you decide to work through the next volume we will spend the months that follow consciously being the capacity for all. As 'no-thing' we will come to see that we can't feel anything about what 'is', we will come to say 'yes' to what happens, and the old judgements will fall away.

The knowledge that you will tear up as you peel this onion, and that the negative feeling should be welcomed for the guidance they give you should make things easier. The expectation that you will experience this dis-ease is an effective defense against the traps ahead. As you practice 'seeing' from your center you will start to see the light beyond, this is the light that will draw you on.

LIVING FROM TRUTH

In the next volume of the 'Way Within' we will be working on living more and more from center. We will be working on living as the one 'no-thing' that we all truly are and exploring living authentically.

Living authentically is in stark contrast to what most of us experience. What most of us experience is akin to living as some worn out fiction that we've been projecting into a world of illusion.

When you are aligned to who you are, you are also in tune with the whole universe. You can't lie anymore. As this alignment comes to fruition you will find that you are content, and your life starts to unfold more fruitfully. In the early stages of practice, you probably won't be aware of the many ways that your life starts to blossom.

At first you might not like what 'is', but that makes no odds. It makes no sense to live your life from what 'is-not', from a fiction. It makes no sense to live an illusion. This initial unease about what 'is' can cloud out the benefits that are coming your way. However, as you embrace what 'is' the blissful benefits will start to color and illuminate all aspects of your life.

SEEING, BEING AND LOVING

At the start of the book I said that the essentials of living an enlightened life are: seeing, being and loving. This book has focused on seeing and we will next turn our attention to being and loving, and the oneness that flows from these.

Being is more than acceptance and authentic living, it is also about our role as co-creators. Being at center, in the now is a creative function, not merely an experience. This is the power that drives the universe and unfolds all that always was. This is about getting out of the way and letting the potential of life flow through you. Your hands, eyes, mouth even your thoughts were always Gods; yet now it's time to get out of the way and let the miracle of creation happen.

Loving, is much more than about forgiveness and acceptance, it's about these for sure but these are just attributes. At a bigger level loving is really about oneness, which is very much an extension of being. Loving is about truth and reality. Once the illusion of fear goes you're only left with Love. Love is all you really are, and Love is all you ever really do.

LIVING AS AWARENESS

You may have started reading this book attached to a sense of being a separate self. In this book, we have looked within to see the spacious capacity at our center. We have talked about this spaciousness as awareness and we have come to see that we are this aware space. We are not a mind in a body where awareness is an attribute of mind. No, our body, mind and all matter are contained in awareness and made from the very same awareness.

Our next task is to embrace our true nature as the knowing of awareness. Our challenge is to live mindfully as awareness. To be authentic.

LIVING IN THE NOW

A major benefit of living from center is that it brings you into the now, it relegates all your failings to ancient history and separates you from their contagion.

The time has come, you have arisen, you have seen the light and you know the truth, now you must be wise and deliver on your promise. It is time to live from awareness to live mindfully.

LIVING IN AMERICA

Writing this book is a key part of my journey home. Much has happened in this process. I started the book living in a small Northamptonshire village, in England. I was a pillar of the society, a Parish councilor, school governor, regular book club member and mower of the village cemetery. I was a good husband, a father of three and lived an idyllic life. Then I moved to New York, spent a couple of years in Connecticut and now find myself living in Manhattan's West Village.

I let go of my country, my family, my friends, my books, my house, my money, my future to find freedom in the unknown. To find myself in America, right here, right where I am.

A word of warning, this was my path, you must find your own path. I would remind you of the story of the sage who when crossing the dessert woke in the morning to find his camels had fled. Asking his acolyte what had happened he was told, "You said trust in Allah, so I trusted Allah to look after the camels." The sage took a very, very long breath then said calmly, "Trust in Allah yes, but tie up the fucking camels."

For years, I feared letting go, but now I know that the only thing to fear, is hanging on to what you never had in any case. I've left many friends behind, and that creates a hole, but the universe is generous and into the void come new friends, new books, and new stories. Of these new friends, I feel blessed to have come to know Claire Scanlon, Anthony Holdampf, Jane Cross, Brian O'Connor, Eric Smith, Walter Denilson, Tricia Farnworth, Lucy Bayly, Nicole, Rosa Esposito, Kevin Baumann, Marie-Jose O'Keefe and Ashley Beverage.

WRITING THE WAY WITHIN

———————— ❦ ————————

BACK IN 2011 I felt that I'd made significant progress in my pursuit of peace and happiness. I had answers to the big questions in my life, I had awareness. I understood the ancient mystical question of "Who am I", and I knew how to help others answer this question for themselves. I was awash with simple techniques that enable people to feel the love, peace and happiness that I felt. Naively, I imagined it would take me nine months to write this book plus a further six months to edit it. Well, it turns out that I was not nearly as aware as I'd imagined, I was at the start of my path and writing this book was to become my way home. In August 2018, or more than six years after I started drafting I finally finished writing it.

Many of my friends and students have read the "Way Within" and been touched. However, I have an awakened friend Nicole, and she chastises me for writing about Awareness. "Why bother", she says. "People get it, or they don't, and everything that needs to be written has been written, end of!"

Despite her smarts, and she is super smart, Nicole misses the point of writing. She doesn't see that writing is a beautiful process where the writer takes all the things in their head and puts them down on paper, then organizes them in a way that makes sense to a reader. As a writer, I create a hierarchy of ideas that propels my reader towards a clear understanding of the subject in a way that benefits both of us.

The writing process is precious because it gently reveals that many of the things in both the reader's and writer's heads are contradictory. Sometimes the contradiction is a question of perspectives, and writing eliminates the problem as the writer carefully brings thoughts and ideas into focus.

Sometimes though, our beliefs fail to make sense when they are laid down next to each other. Our minds have this insane ability to compartmentalize our thinking, we subconsciously create buffers between contradictory views of the world. Our subconscious keeps inconsistent beliefs apart to maintain the illusion of consistency. Compartmentalization is the system that allows us to believe we are sane when quite clearly, we are bonkers. Great writing breaks down these buffers, it can be painful and traumatic but in the end, it should be liberating.

Fortunately for me this laying down of ideas and organizing them over the last six years forced me to reconcile my thinking. I had to understand and then articulate the hidden relationships between the components of the "Way Within". Often, I couldn't find a useful relationship between my ideas. When this happened, I was forced to drop those things that no longer made sense or that didn't fit within the framework of ideas that was developing.

Perhaps most precious of all, the writing process systematically reveals the gaps in an author's understanding. In my case, the gaps emerged as gaping holes in my understanding. If I do my job well then gaps will emerge in the readers understanding too, gaps that together we can start to fill.

The emergence of gaps in our understanding is no bad thing, because if recognized the gaps become the catalyst that makes writing magical, this is where as a writer I come face to face with the void. There is power in not knowing, as soon as you know you have a gap you bring awareness into play, when awareness is at work it's as if the whole universe is conspiring to fill the holes in your understanding. Once you recognize a gap in your understanding your subconscious is always alert for an answer, your subconscious mind is always trying to fill any gaps, and when it finds what you need it brings it to your attention and you recognize it in an instant.

So, having gazed into the emptiness, I often magically meet the very person, discover the book, or find the article that I need to complete the work at hand.

At other times, I see how to join the things I already know in a totally new way. Sometimes and most miraculous of all, the void offers up something totally new and as a writer I am witness to creation.

My understanding of this writing process is that it's not something that I actively do. I don't network, I don't synthesize, and I don't create anything. No, my job as a writer is to get out of the way. My challenge is to wait with a humble open heart and stare into the void ready to catch what is born from this most fertile land. I must wait so that I can give creation a voice and share it with those that will love it, cherish it, and use it.

The point that Nicole missed is that as the writer of this book I was a beneficiary too. Most readers won't get quite as much from a book as the author does from writing it. While writing this book I went from excited optimism to clarity, and then finally arrived at an even deeper love, happiness and peace than I could have previously imagined. I moved down my path and found my way.

It doesn't matter if no one reads this book because it has been transformational for me. However, my hope is that people will read it, and they'll see what it points at so that they can fully enjoy the peace, love and happiness that we are all seeking. I'd love nothing more than to hold your hand as you awaken. Hold your hand as you gaze into the void with an open heart and receive its gifts. I'd love to be there for you as you embrace the truth of your divinely human nature.

There's something else too that escaped Nicole. Each generation is subtly different and needs to find its own language and context for framing spiritual wisdom. Each generation needs to find the truth for itself, each generation needs first-hand experience more than second-hand musings. The book is in your hands now so that you can have first-hand experience of what is.

Soon after starting to write the 'Way Within' it became clear that for completeness there should be two books. One book that deals with awakening and then a second book that tackles how to live an aware life, how to live from and as awareness. This, the first book deals with seeing who you are. It deals with awaking to your truth, it deals with what I mean when I talk about enlightenment. The second deals with living after you have become enlightened, it deals with wisdom.

The second book about living mindfully is doubly necessary as the 'Way Within' is a direct path, so one is likely to experience enlightenment as an instant transformation yet still be left with the baggage from a lifetime of living an unaware life.

Don't despair, carrying baggage after awakening is an inevitable part of taking a direct path. However, as one that walked this way all alone, I know that this can be an overwhelming and confusing time. So, I'm writing the next book to provide support for the freshly awakened seeker as they set out on their own to explore awareness. The irony of course is that in awareness one is never alone. Unlike in everyday life, the 'one' is not one, and yet not two either. Join me in awareness and we will walk together as the one!

Nicole struggles with books like this one because she was never a seeker in the way that I was. She was never a seeker in the way that countless millions of people are seekers. Her awakening was not something she sought, she never had the sense of lack most of us feel, she had a spontaneous awakening, she came to awareness with grace and no effort on her part. She was a freak, she was a Ramana Marharshi, not a Papaji, not a Mooji, not a Buddha or a Jesus like you and me.

In humbleness, I must concede that while the 'Way Within' has been transformational for me and in a multitude of other guises it has been a catalyst for many earlier sages, it is not for everyone.

The truth of self-realization is that it is a non-verbal and non-emotional experience. We are all unique and we all benefit from an approach that is sympathetic to our way of being. Different folks need different strokes. Not just that, but some of us don't want self-realization, some are not quite ready for it, some are ready but need to come at it from a different angle to grasp it.

Regardless of how you get there, the paradox is that after seeing your true nature a myriad of feelings will arise, and you will naturally try to frame the awakening experience in words. However, regardless of the feelings and words the journey is a discovery of your true self. Of this true nature only you are an expert, yet for reasons we will discuss later, this experience will always be beyond words. A trap that keeps many seekers from 'finding' is that they are more attached to words and explanations than they are to the simple knowing of their truth.

Only you can authentically know your truth. So, don't cling to my words or doubt yourself when what you experience and what you feel is different from what other people have described. What you will see will not be what you have imagined and hoped for. It will be far more ordinary and yet at the same time more wonderful than you could imagine. Don't worry if your words are not as poetic or as wise sounding as the mystics. What matters on this journey is that you attend to what you experience not what someone else may write or say.

As you awaken to your true nature, resist the urge to judge others and what they say about this process. We use words to communicate, but words are never the thing. I might talk about spacious capacity, you might talk about openness and your true self. Be free of these words, the words don't matter. What matters is that you look for yourself, what matters is that you embrace your true nature.

Some ways are for some people and other ways are for others. Some people are ready to start their journey home, some are well down the path and others feel no inclination to explore the ways within. Likewise, some people need a guru, some people need to discover their own truth, and some people need to find the way through the power and light of the intellect.

Remember there are many ways and the 'Way Within' is but one, and it might not be one that resonates with your way of being. If you discover that the 'Way Within' is not your way, then at least you have learnt one thing and you will have taken a step away from ignorance and towards the light of awareness.

However, regardless of whether the process encapsulated in the 'Way Within' resonates with you, what is written in this book about both awareness and the problems of seeking is universal, and so there is something for all seekers.

If the 'Way Within' proves fruitful for you, if it proves fruitless, if you have questions, if you have suggestions or if you have comments please feel free to write to me at: Jamie@Spiritbrew.com

A FINAL REQUEST

Please take the time to write a constructive review on Amazon or Goodreads or wherever you purchased the book. Ideally adding a positive review that helps other people see how the book may help them or at least how it helped you. It's always useful for prospective readers if you can say what was unique about this book, how it may benefit people or how it achieves its goals.

ADDITIONAL RESOURCES

TO MAKE FOLLOWING the 'Way Within' easier, Richard Lang has made lots of films that guide you through the headless way exercises and below are the links to these, so you can get more direction and guidance on how to do the exercises and get yourself zero–centric:

http://www.headless.org/videos-experiments.htm

If you get a chance try to join a headless group and attend a workshop in person as this work is much easier when done in good company and with a gentle soul to facilitate it. Check out the 'Way Within' web page for details:

http://www.waywithin.com

There are also some excellent books and my favorites are:

- Awareness by Anthony DeMello
- Awareness Games by Brian Tom O'Connor
- Seeing Who You Really Are by Richard Lang
- The Untethered Soul by Michael A Singer
- Why Materialism Is Baloney by Bernard Kastrup
- Presence Vols 1 & 2 by Rupert Spira
- On Having No Head by Douglas Harding

ACKNOWLEDGEMENTS

IT'S BEEN A long and winding road and I must thank many people. First, I should thank my family starting with my ex-wife Janet who helped me with so much in this book. Thanks to my three children: Libby, Freya and Ben, who never for a moment leave my heart. Thanks to my family, my dad Doug for making me a better person, my mum Heather for being a gentle soul, my sister Peta whose love I can always count on, my brother Martin who I wish I saw more of and my nieces Kirstie, Charlotte and Sophie who I love like sisters.

A special thanks to my seeing friends who are with me on this journey, there have been many of you and all of you brought more than I can say. Of these I will single out those that have walked, with me often showing me the way and pointing out the beautiful views. So, thanks to Anthony, Eliana, Linda Gun, Jane Cross, Nicole, Brian O'Connor, Simon Sutton, Richard Lang and Kam Parmer. A special thank you to Kam, you have been as good a friend as you could ever have, and I know no matter what happened you would always be there in my moment of need, I just wish I had it in me to ask. Special thanks also to Anthony Holdampf who gets everything and put so much thought and care into helping me get this book across the line.

I would like to offer my gratitude and sympathy for my friends that have had to suffer my endless yacking and the quixotic sharing of my stream of consciousness as I spent 7 years writing this book. So, thanks to: Richard Fisher, Neil Simmonite, Scott Mosely, Ashley Beverage, Amanda Ridgeway, Ruth Gaffney, Ian Francis, Rosa Esposito, Karen Woodward, Paul Cowan, Kerrie Smith, Kevin Baumann, William Fawcett and Nigel Fenton.

I should say a thanks to all the people that I've met along the way and all those kind people that have taken the time to read my books. My final thanks go to Claire Scanlon, who is the real deal.

SPIRITBREW PUBLISHING

AT SPIRITBREW WE are interested in helping inspirational and insightful writers connect with an audience that will appreciate and benefit from their ideas and wisdom.

Our goal is to help writers write and reach the widest possible audience. One way we help our writers to write more and work less is by ensuring that our writers retain all the profits from their books. Spiritbrew is not a traditional publisher, we are a collective formed by writers that brings writers together in the belief that we all benefit from sharing platforms, tactics, strategies and an audience. We don't compete as writers we grow, as a collective we all rise together.

ALSO AVAILABLE FROM SPIRITBREW

ANTHONY HOLDAMPF

Anthony Holdampf is a father, entrepreneur and author who resides in New York City. His quest is to experience and acknowledge LOVE, JOY, PEACE, EXPANSION, GRATITUDE and ABUNDANCE and to have others experience the same through interaction with him.

Anthony's book: **Spritbrew – A Man's search for Love, Peace and Purpose through Ayahuasca.**

Anthony thought he had everything, a thriving business, a luxurious home a loving fiancée, and a lavish life style. Then an unexpected encounter with a Shaman would change everything. Desperate and broken after losing everything he travels to Peru on a spiritual quest to find his life's purpose.

During his journey, he encounters many challenges ultimately leading him into the jungles of the Amazon. There with the help of a Shaman and through a series of Ayahuasca ceremonies he begins to understand the forces that have shaped him and ultimately bring him to realizations that will forever change his perspective on life.

SPIRITBREW PAST MASTERS

WE ARE ALSO working hard to bring new editions and new translations of older classic spiritual and inspirational books to a new wider audience.

SPIRITUAL CLASSICS

Our spiritual classics library is made up of timeless classics like the Bhagavad Gita, The Imitation of Christ, The Tao Ching, The Interior Castle, The Enchiridion, The Kybalion, The Upanishads, Siddhartha, Story of a Soul, Cosmic Consciousness, Autobiography of a Yogi, and many, many more.

To get your free copy any of the classics visit:

http://www.spiritbrew.com/

Made in the USA
Columbia, SC
30 October 2020